MW00417220

MONEY

LIFE LESSONS TO HELP YOU PLAN NOW, SAVE WISELY, AND RETIRE WELL

TALKS

Copyright ©2015 by Szarka Financial

Money Talks: Life Lessons to Help You Plan Now, Save Wisely, and Retire Well
by Charles Conrad, JD; Rick Martin, CFP®; Alex Menassa, MT, CPA, JD;
Mark Stratis, CFP®; Les Szarka, CFP®, ChFC®

Published in the United States of America by
Drumm Beat Publishing
www.moneytalksbook.com

ISBN: 978-0-9969145-1-2

All rights reserved. No part of this publication may be reproduced, distributed, or transmitted in any form or by any means, including photocopying, recording, or other electronic or mechanical methods, without the prior written permission of the publisher, except in the case of brief quotations embodied in critical reviews and certain other non-commercial uses permitted by copyright law.

Securities offered through Registered Representatives of Cambridge Investment Research, Inc., a Broker Dealer, member FINRA/SIPC. Advisory Services through Cambridge Investment Research Advisors, Inc., a Registered Investment Adviser. Cambridge and Szarka Financial are not affiliated. Fixed Insurance services offered through Szarka Financial.

Although the author and publisher have made every effort to ensure that the information in this book was correct at time of going to press, the author and publisher do not assume and hereby disclaim any liability to any party for any loss, damage, or disruption caused by errors or omissions, whether such errors or omissions result from negligence, accident, or any other cause.

Project Manager: Kelley Drumm
Developmental Editor: Kelli Christiansen
Cover Designer: Derek Murphy

Szarka Financial
29691 Lorain Road
North Olmsted, OH 44070
www.szarkafinancial.com

Dedication

This book is dedicated to all of those individuals and couples that are looking to plan for their future, to avoid surprises and ultimately retire better than they may have done on their own.

Acknowledgments

The completion of this book could not have been possible without the participation and assistance of so many people that their names cannot be enumerated. Their contributions are sincerely appreciated and gratefully acknowledged. However, the authors would like to express their deep appreciation and indebtedness to the following:

First, we would like to sincerely thank Kelley Drumm for her vision, drive, and commitment to this project. Your leadership and passion for this book, which started as a dream, made it come true!

Next, we would like to express our appreciation to Kelli Christiansen, our Chief Editor, for her commitment to the project and her ability to weave various stories from five different advisors into a cohesive, thoughtful, and enlightening tool for those readers who want to plan, save, and retire well.

We would be remiss without thanking Diana, Chris, Marissa, and Mike (the staff at Szarka Financial), who make us look good every day and who, through their dedication and focus, respond to our clients' needs in an accurate and timely manner.

Finally, we have to thank our clients, families, and friends for sharing their stories with us. The names and identifying details have been changed to protect the privacy of individuals, but the life lessons included in the book would not be as authentic without their help.

Contents

PART III: MANAGE YOUR FUTURE— WHICH BEGINS NOW

Introduction

As we prepared the manuscript for this book, the stock markets were in tumult, riding a roller coaster of ups and downs into correction territory (price declines of at least 10 percent) amid a dramatically slowing economy in China and other countries in Asia, economic uncertainty in Greece and other euro-zone countries, and a still-tenuous recovery in the wake of the Great Recession. Some investors are understandably nervous about swings in the market, especially those who are nearing retirement. Double-digit declines in the stock market could have a dramatic effect on portfolios, especially those heavily weighted in equities.

Tumult in the markets is just one reason why it's so important not only to make a financial plan but to review it frequently and rebalance as necessary. Young individuals and families with a longer investment timeline can carefully choose equities and weather stock market corrections; investors nearing retirement need to think about shifting to fixed-income securities and other less risky investments.

Of course, the stock and bond markets aren't the only venues for investing, and everyone should consider a variety of assets and investment vehicles to help them build their nest eggs in preparation for retirement. Among those considerations are life insurance, long-term care insurance, annuities, trusts, defined-contribution and defined-benefit plans, and so on.

Financial planning goes beyond investing. It also includes paying down debts and loans, saving, creating rainy-day funds, and putting together wills and estate plans designed to protect and preserve your assets.

Regardless of where you are in life—recently out of college, in the middle of your life and career, or nearing your retirement years—good financial planning requires careful considerations that will help you plan for every stage of life, save wisely, and retire well. In these pages, you'll follow the stories of people from many different economic circumstances as they navigate the stages of life. These stories will help illustrate key aspects of financial planning, showing you what to do— and what not to do—as you go through life.

You'll read about Scott* and Teresa, a young couple balancing their day-to-day expenses and massive student loan debt with their desire to buy their first home together. You'll hear about Ted and Alice, a young professional couple about to start a family and considering whether and what kind of insurance they should buy. We'll look at what Mary and John did to use various investment vehicles to their advantage so they could be ready to retire when they reached age 65. You'll see how Sarah navigated a difficult divorce—and learned some tough lessons along the way. We'll look at how Paul and Mary used life insurance and an annuity to fund their golden years. And we'll read about how Jack and Katie navigated the intricacies of Social Security, Medicare, and Medicaid. We'll learn a lot from these and other stories, all of which are taken from real-world examples of dealing with real-life money issues.

Money talks. It says a lot about who we are and who we want to be. It tells us much about how we live our lives. How we deal with money says a lot about our hopes, dreams, and goals. How well we plan for those goals depends in part on how closely we listen to what money is saying. If we don't listen, reaching our financial goals—from buying our first home to taking our dream vacations to retiring comfortably (and everything in between)—can seem almost impossible.

Indeed, planning for retirement can seem a daunting task. Many of us figure that it's so far in the future that we can put off planning until tomorrow. Many of us believe we don't have enough assets to bother creating an estate plan. Some believe that, between our retirement plans and Social Security, we'll have plenty to live on when we quit working.

Ignoring money, putting off financial planning, or avoiding writing a will or planning an estate is never a good idea. It's never smart to assume that everything will work out for the best when it comes to achieving our financial goals, funding our retirements, and preserving our legacies.

In *Money Talks*, we'll tackle these issues, learning from the real-life situations of people just like you. Unfortunately bad things do happen to good people. Throughout the course of this book you will find a number of stories in which life's tragedies struck unexpectedly and see the different impacts those events had on people who had prepared and those who had not. Those lessons will go far in helping you to plan now, save wisely, and retire well.

Please keep in mind that the material and scenarios presented in this book are not financial, tax, legal or investment advice. You should always consider consulting a qualified professional to evaluate your individual circumstances.

---

* All names have been changed to protect privacy.

Part I

Start Now to Help Secure a Lifetime of Financial Freedom

Average American college graduates have about $30,000 in student debt and can expect to earn an entry-level salary of about $45,000 per year.[1] In addition to paying off student loans, most young people also look at paying on average $100 per month for their smartphones, $200 per month in commuting costs, $900 per month for a one-bedroom apartment, and $200 per month in groceries.

Accounting for all of those expenses while trying to build up savings and invest for retirement years—which can seem like a very, very long way off—can be challenging for even the savviest of the Millennial generation. Even so, there are plenty of ways for young individuals and young families to save and invest while using debt wisely and paying off student loans, all with an eye toward the future.

---

[1] Paul F. Campos, "The Real Reason College Tuition Costs So Much," *The New York Times*, April 4, 2015. Retrieved August 25, 2015, from http://www.nytimes.com/2015/04/05/opinion/sunday/the-real-reason-college-tuition-costs-so-much.html?_r=0.

CHAPTER 1

Tackle Student Loan Debt

A frequent trap millions of people have found themselves in is the shocking amounts of student loans they have accumulated. These scenarios are not limited to students but are shared in many cases by well-intentioned parents. Either way, the burden of student loan debt can make it difficult for young individuals and families to start out their new lives right.

In today's highly competitive labor market, a college degree often makes the difference between having the chance to secure financial freedom or living paycheck to paycheck. This is especially true in technical professions such as science, technology, engineering, medicine, accounting, and architecture, where a degree is mandatory.

However, an entire generation of young people has been led to believe that by simply graduating from college, their financial futures could be secured, regardless of the degree earned or the expense incurred earning it. The result is that we now have millions of young adults with college degrees that don't necessarily translate into well-paying jobs. What many do graduate with is tens of thousands of dollars of student loans that they soon find to be difficult, or in some cases impossible, to repay.

Scott and Teresa are a good example of this problem. Both in their late twenties, they got married a few years out of college. Both were working in their chosen fields, Scott as an attorney and Teresa as a nurse practitioner.

The couple had been living in an apartment in a nice suburb for the past few years, but they grew tired of renting and wanted to buy a place of their own and possibly start a family. They knew that buying a house would be difficult on their budget, but they figured it would be better than renting.

They contacted a friend of theirs who was a realtor, and she arranged for them to visit several homes. She also encouraged them to find a mortgage broker who could prequalify them for their purchase.

A few days later, they sat down with a mortgage broker to review their finances. Teresa's income as a nurse practitioner was around $105,000. Scott, on the other hand, was still struggling to find a decent position at a law firm. He had changed jobs a few times already since passing the bar exam, and was working at a very small firm making around $38,000. He had become discouraged at how difficult it had been to find a well-paying position in his chosen field and even considered going back to school to get a master's degree in business.

At first the mortgage broker was encouraged to see that their combined income was more than $140,000, and he figured they wouldn't have any problem qualifying for a mortgage. But things started to unravel when he asked them how much debt they were carrying. Scott informed him that he had student loans of $220,000. The look of surprise on the mortgage broker's face turned to shock when Teresa added that her student loans totaled $210,000. The mortgage broker couldn't believe what he was hearing: This couple, still in their twenties, had already accumulated more than $430,000 in debt. They'd be paying more than $3,200 a month for twenty years—just on their student loans.

As he examined their finances in more detail, the mortgage broker found that their combined income of $143,000 left them a net monthly income of $7,900 after taxes and medical premiums. More than 40 percent of their income was going toward paying off their student loans. Two car payments added another $700 per month to their bills. This left about $4,000 a month to pay for all their rent, utilities, food, insurance, and other miscellaneous expenses. No wonder they were finding it difficult to put any money into savings and their 401(k) plans.

Scott and Teresa were disappointed when the broker informed them they would not qualify for the loan amount they needed to buy their dream home. They could still get a house if it was at half the price of the homes they had been looking at. Their student loan debt was crushing them—and their dreams of home ownership.

How do people fall into this student loan trap? The schools themselves are a big part of the problem. The cost of a higher education has increased twice as fast as the price of other goods and services. For this, the colleges have no one to blame but themselves. For years colleges and universities have passed along escalated costs to their students, with little effect on enrollment. By some measures, the cost of college has multiplied exponentially: "[O]ver the past 35 years, college tuition at public universities has nearly quadrupled, to $9,139 in 2014 dollars."[2] Private institutions cost even more: "Today, the average sticker price of a private four-year college is $42,419."[3] One of the reasons colleges have been able to raise tuition with little ill effect has been the relative ease by which students could get loans. As their costs escalated, colleges simply encouraged students who couldn't afford to pay tuition to load up on easily obtainable student loans.

Most students who take out loans are in their late teens to early mid-twenties. The vast majority of these young people have little or no prior experience with taking on debt, and so they often don't have a full appreciation of the consequences. Many student loans are "deferred payment loans," meaning that no payments are due until after graduation. Typically there is no immediate monthly payment due upon securing the loan to remind them of the debt they are accumulating while they're in school.

---

[2]   Paul F. Campos, "The Real Reason College Tuition Costs So Much," *The New York Times*, April 4, 2015. Retrieved August 25, 2015, from http://www.nytimes.com/2015/04/05/opinion/sunday/the-real-reason-college-tuition-costs-so-much.html?_r=0.

[3]   Jeffrey J. Selingo, "Just How High Can College Tuition Go?" *The Washington Post*, March 2, 2015. Retrieved August 25, 2015, from http://www.washingtonpost.com/news/grade-point/wp/2015/03/02/just-how-high-can-college-tuition-go/.

For many, their student loan debt continues to grow, even though they might not realize it. With a deferred loan, interest payments are not forgiven; rather, the amount owed simply accumulates with interest until graduation, and the total interest is added to the original loan amount. So an original first-year loan could be 20 percent higher by the time a student graduates after four years, or 30 percent higher for a student who goes on to get a master's degree. Such was the case with Scott and Teresa. About 25 percent of their total student loan balances was simply deferred interest.

The schools are only part of the problem, however. Students and their parents are equally at fault for the student loan crisis we have in our country. (It is a crisis: in the United States alone, there's about $1.2 trillion in outstanding student loan debt, about $40 billion of which has reached "junk" status.)[4] Many students have incurred huge student loans, only to leave school before getting their degree, or in some cases, earned degrees that might not lead to a job that pays enough to justify the cost of debt incurred.

Special consideration should be made regarding the amount of tuition and debt a student is willing to incur relative to the potential income from their chosen field or profession. Some occupations that are noble in cause unfortunately do not pay as much as others. While personal satisfaction from a chosen profession is important, it has to be balanced against the financial pressure arising from an excessive amount of debt incurred by pursuing that degree.

When it comes to taking on student loan debt, if you are a college-bound student you should research your chosen field, for instance, the typical salary for an entry-level position. Based on the average starting pay, calculate whether you could afford the monthly payments on the total debt you may need to incur in order to get your degree or certificate. You may want to consider limiting the monthly payment on the total student loans you incur to between 10 percent and 15 percent of your gross starting pay.

---

[4]   Jody Shenn and Matt Scully, "$40 Billion of AAA Student Loans Are at Risk of Becoming Junk," *Bloomberg Business*, July 1, 2015. Retrieved August 25, 2015, from http://www.bloomberg.com/news/articles/2015-07-15/america-s-student-loan-crisis-risks-turning-aaa-debt-into-junk.

For example, if the starting pay for a chosen occupation is $40,000/ year, 10 to 15 percent of the gross pay would be between $335/month and $500/month. This amount is a reasonable monthly payment for a student loan, and the payments could support total student loans of approximately $47,000 to $70,000.

Basically, 10 percent of a $40,000 occupation could support total debt of $47,000, while 15 percent could support student loans of about $70,000. The choice between the two amounts of debt comes down to how much of your lifestyle you are willing to give up in order to repay your student loans. One major exception to this rule would be if the anticipated income of the profession increases sharply over a relatively short period of time. Physicians are an example of this.

In order to mitigate the high costs of student loan debt, consider attending a community college for the first one or two years pursuing a bachelor's degree. This could dramatically reduce the total cost of your education and the subsequent debt you may need to incur. Remember, people typically ask you where you graduated from, not where you went for your first two years, so attending a community college for your freshman and sophomore years and then transferring to a four-year institution for your junior and senior years can save money in both tuition and room and board (many students who attend two-year community colleges live at home during those years). In fact, according to the College Board, "the average cost of tuition and fees at a two-year school is only $3,131, just over one third of the cost for a year at a four-year public institution."[5] This means that, by attending a community college for two years, you could save anywhere from about $15,000 to more than $62,000 depending on whether you were to attend a public four-year institution or a private university.[6]

---

[5]   Christina Couch, "Two-Year vs. Four-Year Colleges: Which One Is Right for You?" *CollegeView.com*, n.d. Retrieved August 24, 2015, from http://www.collegeview.com/articles/article/two-year-vs-four-year-colleges-which-one-is-right-for-you

[6]   The College Board, "Average Published Undergraduate Charges by Sector, 2014–15," *The College Board Annual Survey of Colleges*, n.d. Retrieved August 24, 2015, from http://trends.collegeboard.org/college-pricing/figures-tables/average-published-undergraduate-charges-sector-2014-15

Another option to consider is to start early acquiring college credits, which also can help reduce the costs of college. Many high school districts offer postsecondary options for their students. This allows students to take classes at certain colleges while still in high school. These programs allow students to earn college credits while still in high school, sometimes one or even two years' worth of college credits. Best of all, there typically is no cost to the student for taking college classes as part of such programs. This can be a cost-effective way to earn credits toward a four-year degree.

Whether student loans are taken out to cover the cost of two-year institutions or four-year institutions or graduate school, it's important to pay them off as quickly as possible. New graduates (and, if applicable, their parents) should sit down and take a close—and honest—look at all their revenues and expenses and craft a realistic budget that incorporates student-loan payments. Unless you have other credit card debt at substantially higher interest rates, if possible, consider paying an extra $100 or $200 each month in order to pay down student loans as quickly as possible. This might require taking on a part-time job to supplement income from your day job. It might require putting off buying that new car. It very likely will require some serious budgeting.

Despite rising costs, college remains a solid investment for most people.[7] The challenge is in avoiding the kind of crushing student loan debt that makes your first few years in the "real world" a financial nightmare. By weighing the cost of student loans against anticipated annual income, young people will be better positioned to start out after college with fewer financial burdens. Living with as little debt as possible makes life a whole lot easier. We'll look at that next, in Chapter 2.

---

[7] Mark Peters and Douglas Belkin, "Surprising Findings on Two-Year vs. Four-Year Degrees," *The Wall Street Journal*, June 24, 2014. Retrieved August 24, 2015, from http://www.wsj.com/articles/fed-study-says-it-still-makes-sense-to-go-to-college-1403618488

Lessons Learned

- Student loan debt can add up, especially when considering deferred payments and compounded interest, all of which can boost the cost of the loan. As a result, some graduates find that as much as 40 percent of their annual income is eaten up by student loan payments.

- When taking on student loan debt, a good rule of thumb is to limit the monthly payment on the total student loans you incur to between 10 percent and 15 percent of the anticipated gross average annual income in your chosen field.

- Attending community college for the first two years of your university career and then transferring to a four-year institution can save you thousands of dollars in tuition and room and board, thereby reducing the overall debt you might incur by taking out student loans.

CHAPTER 2

Get a Handle on Debt and Loans

As though crushing student loan debts weren't enough, many people often find themselves in the unfortunate situation of having high credit card balances—and wonder how they got there. By the time they fully grasp the trap they have fallen into, they might already be drowning in debt and struggling to pay the excessive monthly payments that go along with it.

How do so many people fall into this insidious debt trap? Easily.

Imagine that, while at work one day, your boss informs you that because of the great job you've been doing, you will be receiving a $1,000 bonus on your next paycheck. "Great!" you think. There have been some things you've been putting off buying because finances at home have been tight lately. So you go home and excitedly tell your wife about your windfall.

Let's say that you've been driving your car on four well-worn tires, and it's way overdue for new ones. So you go to the tire store, where a salesman convinces you that for only $500 more, you can upgrade your old, boring hubcaps to sporty new ones. The total bill is $1,200, but with the $1,000 check coming in a few weeks, that shouldn't be a problem. You think, "What the heck—it will really only cost me a couple hundred dollars, right?" And, besides, your new hubcaps will make the car look great! So you put the new tires and hubcaps on your credit card, and you tell yourself you'll just pay it off when the bonus check arrives in a few weeks.

In the meantime, your wife has been planning to do something special for your anniversary. So she decides to surprise you by booking a short junket to Las Vegas for the two of you. The $1,300 is more than she was planning to spend, but with the $1,000 bonus check coming, it really is only going to cost a few hundred bucks. And, besides, it's your anniversary! So she puts it on the credit card and figures she'll just pay it off with the bonus check.

A few days later the two of you are sitting in your living room watching TV. It's the 26-inch set your aunt got you as your wedding gift five years ago. Just then a commercial comes on and you see Crazy Eddie advertising a brand-new, 52-inch, 3D HDTV for only $1,100. And, if you order by credit card, it will be shipped directly to your house within twenty-four hours. As if that isn't enough, if you order in the next thirty minutes, you will get a cappuccino maker at no extra charge! You look at each other, and almost simultaneously say, "Gee, with that bonus check coming in, the TV would almost be free! And, besides, we love cappuccino!"

You can guess what happens next.

A few weeks later that bonus appears in your paycheck: $740. What happened to the $1,000? Taxes.

That evening, when you sit down to pay your bills, you open your credit card statement, which now shows a balance of $3,600—the tires and hubcaps, the Las Vegas anniversary junket, and the new TV. It'll take you the better part of a year to pay down the balance. The worst part is all you have now is $740.

Later that evening you sit down with your wife to tell her the bad news. Between what both of you spent, and including the interest on your credit card, your bonus ended up costing you $3,175. You both decide that if you tighten your belt, you should be able to pay the balance off in nine months or so. Let's just hope there are no other bonuses in the meantime—you can't afford them!

Many people have trouble budgeting and controlling their spending. In fact, the average American household carries a credit card balance of more than $15,000.[8] We live in a society that says "I want it, and I want it now!" And it's easy to yield to this mantra since most of our transactions are done electronically and not with cash. For some it doesn't seem to matter if they don't have the money to buy an item; they simply use a credit card. With credit cards and debit cards, we never have to witness any cash actually leaving our hands—or our bank accounts.

With electronic transactions, we lose the real cost of a purchase because we're paying for it theoretically. It's a lot easier to buy that new iPhone for $400 when you can pay for it on a credit card, because it really didn't cost you anything today (at least not in your mind). If you had to peel off forty $10 bills to pay for it, you might think twice before buying it, because you'd have $400 less in your pocket. But when you use plastic, there's no pain associated with your purchases. When there's no pain associated with spending money, it can be difficult to stick to a budget—because your budget becomes an abstract notion with money never actually leaving your hands.

If you have trouble budgeting or have a spending problem, one of the most effective ways to curb unnecessary spending is to use cash whenever possible. Once a week or before you go shopping, decide how much you can afford to spend and then go to the bank and withdraw that amount in cash—and only that amount. Doing so allows you to establish what you can afford, and it's an effective mechanism that will automatically tell you when you have to stop: you can't buy anything if you can't pay for it with cash. You'll likely find that as the week goes by and your cash begins to dwindle, you'll be less tempted to buy frivolous things (like a $5 iced decaf, extra-shot café latte), because once the cash is gone, it's gone. On the other hand, if you buy everything on a credit or debit card, there is no physical reminder to stop.

This isn't to say that all debt is bad. There is "smart debt" and "dumb debt." Smart debt includes investments such as a home, business, or education.

---

[8]   Tim Chen, "American Household Credit Card Debt Statistics: 2015," *Nerd Wallet*, n.d. Retrieved August 24, 2015, from http://www.nerdwallet.com/blog/credit-card-data/average-credit-card-debt-household/

Using debt to finance an asset expected to appreciate, such as a house, is usually a good use of your money. After the debt is paid off, you ideally would have an asset that was worth more than what you originally paid for it, and along the way it provided you with shelter.

Another smart use of debt could be to purchase an asset that will produce income for you, such as a business, a new piece of machinery, or an apartment building. The income produced by the asset would eventually pay for the loan and, hopefully, generate a profit over time.

A third example may be to use student loans to help finance an education that leads to a well-paying career. An important note here is to weigh the cost of the loan against expected income, as we discussed in Chapter 1. For example, the additional income from a better job gained as a result of earning an MBA should eventually pay for the student loan.

These are just a few examples of how using debt intelligently can help you improve your life responsibly. People who use debt wisely not only use it for smart reasons but also make sure they can either pay off the entire balance every month or, at the very least, make the minimum payment on time every month.

Unfortunately, some people use debt foolishly. This is dumb debt. In some cases, people use debt to finance a lifestyle that they really can't afford. In those instances, the money they earn is not enough to pay their bills and cover their purchases. Instead of changing their spending habits, they simply use their credit cards or other debt to make up the difference. Eventually this kind of debt may end up ruining their lives.

For instance, let's say that you, like the average American household, are carrying $15,000 in credit card debt. Let's further assume that you're making only the minimum monthly payment, which, at the average credit card interest rate of 18 percent would be about $500. At that rate, it would take you more than sixteen years to pay off the entire balance, and in addition to the charges you put on the card yourself, you'd be paying an extra $9,000 in interest.

As you can see, using credit cards to finance a lifestyle you couldn't otherwise afford is never a good idea. As a rule, your monthly cash flow should determine your spending and lifestyle. That doesn't mean you should never use credit cards. It can make sense, for example, to use credit cards for emergencies or large, unexpected bills or purchases, such as for a car repair or a broken appliance. But remember: if you have already maxed out credit cards on frivolous things, you might not be able to use credit when you need it the most.

Furthermore, carrying large balances on your credit cards, particularly if you start missing payments, can damage your credit score and, consequently, make it difficult or more expensive to secure other debt such as auto loans or mortgages. Missing payments also can result in hefty late fees and increased interest rates, both of which further add to your debt.

Establishing good credit and learning how to use credit and debt wisely are important for any number of reasons. Your credit score can affect everything from interest rates on student loans, auto loans, and credit cards to what you pay for mortgage or rent. Of course, the amount of debt you carry also affects you in other obvious ways, including the balance of your checking and savings accounts and how well you can afford to meet your daily expenses.

When the last chapter is written as to the main cause of the decline of the American financial dream, credit cards will likely be at the top of the list of culprits. Credit cards allow (some might even say "encourage") people to live lifestyles they otherwise couldn't really afford. Unfortunately, by the time most people realize what has happened to them, they have dug a hole that is too deep to get out of without suffering a lot of pain.

Paying off those debts as quickly as possible will alleviate that pain. Although it might hurt for a while, sticking to a strict budget, living within your means, and paying down existing debts and loans will make you feel a whole lot better in the long run. And it will better position you to make your money work for you—instead of you working so hard for your money (and then watching it slip through your fingers so quickly). We'll look at that next, in Chapter 3.

Lessons Learned

- In order to avoid amassing hefty credit card balances and other debt, it's important to establish a budget and stick to it. It can be helpful to live on a cash-only basis for everyday expenses, using credit cards only for large or unexpected expenses.

- High credit card balances can take years to pay off and end up costing you thousands of extra dollars in interest fees. In order to avoid wasting money on paying down debt, be sure to pay as much as possible beyond the monthly minimum payment.
- Late or missed credit card payments can be damaging to your credit score, which can negatively impact the cost of other loans (e.g., student loans, car loans, mortgages), keep you from securing other debt, and even negatively influence your background screening for many employers and landlords.

CHAPTER 3

Make Your Money Work for You

Most people work hard for their paychecks. Many have to fight traffic and bad weather, and put up with lazy or uncooperative coworkers, bossy supervisors, and unrealistic workloads, all in the name of getting a paycheck at the end of the week.

Before some of us even get a chance to spend a single dime of our hard-earned wages, it seems like there is an endless number of people waiting in line who want their unfair share. Many of us watch as our paychecks get gobbled up by student loan debt and credit card bills. After Social Security taxes, federal taxes, state taxes, local taxes, union dues, health insurance premiums, and other benefit deductions are subtracted, it's easy to feel as though half the week is spent working for free. No wonder the average American family has so much trouble putting anything aside for savings or retirement.

Craig and Gina are a young couple in their late twenties who feel like their finances are moving backward. Although they both make nice livings as software programmers, having a combined income of $145,000 per year, they don't feel like they are saving enough toward their retirement goals. Because of Gina's own health issues and her family's poor health history, they are hoping to retire by the time they get to age 55. They want to have enough quality years in retirement in the event her health condition worsens.

Craig and Gina bought their home less than a year ago, and the $1,200/month they had been saving toward their down payment is now being redirected into their savings account. The account pays only 0.5 percent interest, and to add insult to injury, they have to pay taxes on the interest.

They decided they needed to do something to try to get more out of their money. They identified strategies to keep more of their income, protect their savings from being taxed a second time, and make their money work a little harder for them.

First, they redirected $1,200 per month of what they were putting into their savings account into their employer's 401(k) plans. When they were saving aggressively toward a down payment on their new house, they never bothered to get any information about the company's plan. They discovered that the company would match up to 6 percent of whatever they put into the plan. In addition, the $1,200 per month would be deducted from their paychecks before taxes are calculated, so they would save more than $4,600 in taxes per year. Furthermore, anything the 401(k) account earned during the year would not be taxed. This one simple change put an additional $19,000 every year into their retirement savings: $14,400 in the company's 401(k) match plus $4,600 in tax savings.

Second, they started contributing to their company's health savings account (HSA). During the course of a year, Craig and Gina spent more than $4,000 in out-of-pocket medical expenses. The money they spent on glasses, medications, and supplements for Gina's medical condition came from after-tax dollars. By having $4,000 withheld from their paychecks and redirected into their HSAs, they were able to cover some medical expenses before taxes. This saved them an additional $1,200 per year in taxes.

Third, they moved a portion of their savings account that was taxable interest into tax-free bonds. Although the investment was riskier than the savings account, this was money they felt they would not need for at least ten years, putting time on their side to take on more risk. The combination of earning potentially higher interest, tax free, was a welcome surprise.

Fourth, they redirected $4,000 of their combined year-end bonuses into their 401(k) plan. In the past, they would have simply put the money after it was taxed into their savings account. Putting $4,000 of it into their defined-contribution retirement plans saved them an additional $1,300 per year in taxes. Even though the company did not match this portion of the contribution, it was still well worth the tax savings.

Craig and Gina also had additional pleasant surprises when they filed their tax returns. At the time they purchased their home, their mortgage and tax payments were approximately $300 per month more than what they had been paying in rent, an amount they figured would come out of their planned savings. Instead, they discovered that between the tax deductions for the mortgage interest and the property taxes, their after-tax housing costs were almost exactly the same as their rent. This meant that they actually had an additional $300 per month more income than they had originally planned.

The other bit of good news was an additional $750 savings on their taxes by filing their returns separately instead of jointly, taking advantage of their deductions and Gina's medical expenses. (If married, it always makes sense to run your tax calculations both ways in order to make sure that you aren't passing up any tax savings.) In addition, there were some charitable contributions that they forgot to deduct.

By making some small changes and taking advantage of existing benefits and tax-saving techniques, Craig and Gina were able to save an additional $22,000 per year of real money. Investigating some simple strategies to make their money work harder for them paid off in tangible ways, allowing them to take important steps toward securing the financial freedom they desired for their retirement.

Making your money work harder for you is a good first step in laying a foundation to pursue a secure financial future. It's important to save as much as you can, and reducing your overall tax bill through before-tax benefits is a useful tool. Also important is investing wisely, and we'll look at that next, in Chapter 4.

Lessons Learned

- Take advantage of your employer's benefits package, especially anything that is available on a before-tax basis. This includes

HSAs and your employer's defined-contribution plan, to which you should contribute as least as much as the company will match.

- Take full advantage of all the tax breaks available to you. The tax laws are confusing and continually changing, and it's easy to miss some valuable deductions. Many times the money you save on your taxes will be much more than the amount you would spend to have them done professionally.

- When deciding to either rent or buy a home, take into account all the relevant variables and total costs, including utilities, homeowners' dues or assessments, maintenance, potential out-of-pocket expenses, and tax deductions. There is no standard rule of thumb as to whether renting or owning is better; it really depends on your individual circumstances.

CHAPTER 4

Make the Most of Your Longer Time Horizon

Making your money work harder for you can go a long way to providing the extra money needed to both fuel your savings and allow you to move beyond basic savings and checking accounts to other investments with heftier returns. While it takes some discipline and it is not done without sacrifice, there can be tremendous payback when a young person starts a savings and investment plan. How you invest can make a huge difference when you have time on your side.

The power of compounded earnings is one of the biggest draws to investing early, as is clearly evident when compound earnings result in a high investment return over the long term. A method for estimating the number of years required to double your money at a given interest rate is the Rule of 72. Divide 72 by the interest rate (which earns compound interest over the investment period). The result is the approximate number of years that it will take for your investment to double.

Take as an example a $10,000 investment. At earnings of 6 percent per year, it will take approximately 12 years (72/6 = 12) to double the investment to $20,000. In contrast, at earnings of 3 percent per year, it will take approximately 24 years (72/3 = 24) to double your money.

Let's consider another example that illustrates how important it is for young people to begin investing as soon as possible. At 25, Thomas began investing $250 at the beginning of every month in a tax-deferred 401(k) account and his employer matched the contribution with an additional $125 (some employers offer to contribute a 50 percent match up to a limit, usually 5 to 6 percent of salary). If Thomas continues this contribution, he will accumulate $984,305 by age 65 if the funds grow at 7 percent per year, which is the historic average annual return in the U.S. stock market. In contrast, if he earns only 3 percent over that same period, it will only grow to $347,272, a difference of $637,033.

Let's take another more detailed look at the power of investing from a young age. Rachel was single, 23 years old, and college educated when she began a good job at a major corporation. Her benefits included a 50 percent employer match up to 6 percent of her contributions to her 401(k) plan. Her employer is located in a major metropolitan area where living expenses are relatively high.

By age 25, Rachel had learned to manage all of her expenses and was ready to start saving. She understood the value of putting away a few dollars every month, using the power of compound earnings, and investing in the stock market to grow her portfolio, especially when starting at a young age. Although concerned about the two major corrections to the U.S. stock market since 2000 (in 2000–02 and 2008–09), she saw that, over the long term, the market has recovered from every major correction and proceeded to set new highs in subsequent years.

Although past performance is no guarantee of future results, Investopedia.com states that, "According to historical records, the average annual return for the S&P 500 since its inception in 1928 through 2014 is approximately 10 percent." As she started to develop her savings and investment plan, Rachel demonstrated an interesting perspective. She was comfortable allocating her 401(k) contributions to the stock market. In fact, she invested 100 percent of her contributions and the corporate match to an S&P 500 index fund. This is a fairly risky approach, but one she could afford since she had many years before retirement when she would need to access the funds in her 401(k).

Rachel took a different approach with her individual savings, however. She did not want to put that money at risk, so she kept it in the bank in a savings account. She said that she did not actually see the pretax money that was contributed to the 401(k), so she was comfortable putting it at risk. But since she had paid taxes on the money she received in her paycheck, she felt differently about risking that money in the stock and bond markets.

Rachel had done some research and discovered the Roth IRA, another valuable investment tool for young investors. Combining compound earnings within a Roth IRA can make a huge difference over time. The Roth IRA was established by the Taxpayer Relief Act of 1997 and named for its chief legislative sponsor, Senator William Roth of Delaware. It originally allowed individuals to invest up to $2,000 in an account with no immediate tax relief, but provided that the earnings could later be withdrawn tax-free at retirement. The amount that can be contributed to a Roth IRA has increased over time, but now there are income thresholds that limit who is eligible to contribute.

Rachel decided to put some of her after-tax money into a Roth IRA. This makes tremendous sense for young people, because they are usually in a lower tax bracket early in their career, so getting a tax deduction is not that important, making a Roth IRA more valuable. When Rachel reaches retirement and begins to withdraw from the Roth IRA, all of the original investment and the earnings are withdrawn tax free.

Rachel could be quite pleased in the future when she looks back at what she has saved and earned over the course of her life. For example, if she saves $2,000 per year for 40 years, she will have contributed $80,000 ($2,000 × 40 = $80,000). If her contributions earn an average annual return of 5 percent, she would have $161,600 in earnings. Her Roth IRA could be worth $241,600 ($80,000 + $161,600 = $241,600). In any other type of account, she would face a significant tax bill on those gains when she withdraws funds. However, with a Roth IRA, all distributions, including earnings, are withdrawn tax free. At retirement, she can withdraw the entire amount and owe zero taxes!

That potential may be enough to convince Rachel to continue with her savings plan and possibly increase the amount that she saves each month as her income increases over time. To further enhance her returns, if she were able to increase her annual average return from 6 percent to 7 percent, the Roth IRA balance would increase from $241,600 to $399,270. The potential for that kind of increase might motivate her to take on more risk by increasing her investments in stocks and bonds. We'll discuss this next, in Chapter 5.

Lessons Learned

- Investing over the long haul can provide lasting benefits that go far to funding a comfortable retirement. The earlier you start investing, the more time you have to take advantage of the wonders of compounding, which will help your investments grow exponentially.

- Investing in a 401(k) or other company-sponsored defined-contribution plan as early as possible will help you grow your portfolio. Adding to your 401(k) is usually relatively painless because deposits are made directly from your paycheck on a pretax basis.

- Savings accounts, 401(k) plans, Roth IRAs, and other vehicles are valuable investing tools that can help younger investors get started on building their portfolios. All investors should consider time horizons, risk levels, and retirement goals when choosing appropriate investments to help them build a comfortable nest egg.

CHAPTER 5

Invest in Your Future

Establishing savings accounts, putting money into defined-contribution plans, and building up assets are important parts of laying a solid foundation to help to pursue a secure financial future so that you can retire well. But when it comes to saving for—and investing in—the future, young individuals and families should consider avenues beyond company-sponsored 401(k) plans and actively invest in the markets.

Investing in the markets, whether it's the stock, bond, real estate, or precious metal (e.g., gold, silver, copper) markets, exposes your money to risk. Certain markets have more risk than others, but risk and reward go hand in hand with one another. You won't be rewarded by any of these markets unless you take risk. Generally, riskier markets provide higher rewards but also expose the investor to higher potential losses as well. So, how much risk should you be taking? The answer to this question depends on a variety of factors. In general, the younger you are, the more risk you can afford to take.

There may be several good reasons for making the last statement, but the most compelling reason for taking more risk when you are young is that you have time on your side. The younger you are, the longer your investment timeline to recover from any major market corrections and subsequent losses you might endure.

Generally speaking, all U.S. and many foreign investment markets have grown in value over a rolling ten-year period more often than not, despite extended periods of lackluster growth or even loss. Individual investors in their twenties or thirties who put money into any of these markets should see their account values grow over twenty-five to forty years. Diversifying investments by placing a portion of the total investment portfolio in several different markets and asset classes (a technique often referred to as "asset allocation") helps reduce the possibility of a total loss, though it also can reduce the overall growth. Based on historical market returns, if you have the time and discipline, you could see a 6 percent to 8 percent average growth per year over an extended period.

Of course, past performance is no guarantee of future results, and today's markets can be more volatile than ever. The world has never been so connected. Information flows more quickly around the globe—almost instantaneously. World events can have an instant impact on world markets, sometimes positive and sometimes negative.

For example, on August 24, 2015, according to theguardian.com, Chinese markets dropped 8.5 percent on one day, which sent ripple effects around the world: markets tumbled, down 4 percent in Japan, 4 percent in Australia, and more than 4.6 percent in Europe. In the United States, the Dow Jones Industrial Average dropped more than 1,000 points before rebounding and ending down 588 points or 3.5 percent.

Unrest in a country like China, which is home to the world's second largest economy, can cause jitters around the world. Most investors like slow and steady growth, and volatility typically makes investors unsure of what might occur next. Furthermore, the markets might not perform as they have in the past. Social, political, and economic events can apply pressure to the investment community as well. Some investors feel uneasy with this kind of volatility, but some are comfortable with the associated risks because they understand that volatility evens out over longer time horizons.

Another key issue for young investors to consider is how to balance inflation against investment risk. Inflation reduces the future purchasing power of today's dollar. As inflation increases the prices of goods and services in the future, fixed-income sources lose purchasing power over time. If your savings and investments don't make more than the rate of inflation, then you can't buy as much as you did in the past, which reduces your standard of living. According to InflationData. com, inflation historically has averaged around 3 percent, but it has been below that figure in the United States since 2012. At some point, prices of everyday goods and services will start to increase again, fueling inflation. When that occurs, interest rates likely will increase as well, along with wages, which might motivate young families to consider taking more investment risk in order to grow their assets more quickly.

In order to build enough assets to support their retirement plan, young individuals or families either need to save more money or consider taking on additional risk. In most cases, they want their assets to grow faster and higher than the rate of inflation, but they also want to guard against significant losses. A portfolio with exposure to different sectors of the market can reduce the overall impact of any particular loss, but also can reduce potential gains.

By way of illustrating this, let's consider two couples with two very different investment strategies.

Melissa and Andy are both 28 years old. They expect to work until they are 66 years old. They are contributing 6 percent to their respective 401(k) plans and receiving a 3 percent match from their employers. They both have worked for the past six years and selected an aggressive investment portfolio. Rather than worry about protecting their portfolio against short-term losses, they chose a portfolio that invests 90 percent of their contributions in the stock market (60 percent U.S. and 30 percent international) and 10 percent in a U.S. bond fund. Their account has grown tremendously during the past six years as the U.S. stock market, represented by the S&P 500, has grown more than 80 percent from September 1, 2009 to September 1, 2015, according to finance.yahoo.com. The markets will experience a significant correction again, and when they do, Melissa and Andy will likely see a similar drop in the total value of their investment portfolio. However, they aren't worried because they know that they're still contributing to their portfolio, and, so, when the market drops, they have an opportunity to buy more investments at lower prices. It's like a sale at Nordstrom's! Melissa and Andy know that it is highly likely that the value of their portfolio will vary greatly over the next thirty-eight years until it's time for them to retire, but they are comfortable taking the short-term losses in exchange for the higher long-term gains they hope to see in the future.

On the other hand, Charlotte and Spencer are much more conservative. They watched their parents lose a lot of money in the 2000–02 stock market correction, so they had no plans to participate in the stock market. Instead, they chose a more conservative path. Like Melissa and Andy, they both contribute 6 percent of their salaries to their corporate 401(k) plans and receive a 3 percent match from the employers. But unlike them, they decided to invest very conservatively, choosing an aggregate bond fund. Since the match provides a 50 percent gain on their contributions, they still will be growing their funds for eventual retirement. It is not likely that they will see their balance grow as fast as Melissa and Andy, but nor will they see as much volatility in their account balance. They feel good about the fact that their savings are protected in the event of a market meltdown, even though they might not earn enough to outpace inflation over the long term.

Only time will tell who has the better strategy. There is no right answer here. Each individual or family needs to find the strategy that best fits them. An investment strategy should take into consideration long-term financial goals, annual savings, and portfolio risk. Once long-term financial goals are established, then a projected return based on how much risk the portfolio is exposed to can be used to estimate the annual savings required to achieve the goals.

Risk is part of life. How much risk you're willing to take depends on a lot of things, so the avenues you use to invest in the markets is something you should consider carefully—but investing in the markets is still something you really should do, whether conservatively or more aggressively. You also should consider other financial planning tools, including insurance. We'll tackle that next, in Chapter 6.

Lessons Learned

- It's crucial for young individuals and young families to consider a variety of investment vehicles, going beyond

31

company-sponsored plans like 401(k)s to stocks, bonds, mutual funds, and real estate.

- Even if you decide to restrict your investments to your 401(k) or other company-sponsored plan, be sure to diversify across and within investment vehicles, for instance, making sure not to weight your portfolio too heavily in stocks or in U.S.–based assets.

- Younger investors have a longer investment timeline and so, theoretically, can take on more risk. But how much risk you're comfortable with is an individual decision. Even so, you should look for investments that will earn a rate of return that beats inflation.

CHAPTER 6

Make Insurance Part of Your Financial Plan

Savings accounts, 401(k) accounts, investment portfolios—it can be fun to watch these assets grow over time, accumulating wealth as you save wisely so you can retire well. Of course, there are other financial planning tools that can help you plan now, and insurance is one of them.

Insurance is one of those things that most of us rarely think about or think about begrudgingly. Insurance isn't as sexy as the stock market. Insurance is something we have to get, sometimes as a civil mandate, like state laws requiring auto insurance, or as a mortgage requirement, like homeowners insurance. Some of us get renters insurance. But most of us don't think beyond these protections—and that's a mistake. Insurance is an effective financial tool that can help preserve assets and protect legacies.

At some point in life, most of us have to make decisions about insurance. Three basic categories encompass a person's insurance needs: property and casualty insurance to cover home and auto; life and disability income insurance; and health and medical insurance. Although some people consider purchasing insurance risky (there's a chance you might never need it), the real danger is in buying the wrong kind of insurance.

For most of us, our exposure to insurance often begins with the requirement to purchase auto insurance in order to meet state minimums and to renew drivers' licenses. The next consideration is usually medical insurance, when, for instance, newly minted graduates are no longer on either a university healthcare plan or their parents' insurance plans and find their first full-time jobs. Entry-level employees often face questions regarding the benefits package offered by their employers, which typically includes a discussion of medical coverage and deductibles.

The need to purchase insurance then continues to move at a pretty consistent pace, and soon enough prompts a kitchen-table conversation about the need for homeowners or renters insurance, life insurance, disability income insurance, and even long-term care insurance.

The decision-making process usually follows the same trajectory or pattern for most people. A phone call or letter is received suggesting that the time has come for a decision regarding the purchase of life insurance. What do you do?

Most of us have shirked communication with the Ned Ryersons of the world (the pushy insurance guy from the movie *Groundhog Day*). We know we need auto coverage, for example, but what kind and how much? We might have an inkling that renters insurance can protect some of the valuables in our apartment, but most of us figure that we're just renting and so why bother? Some of us buy insurance for our cell phones. Some of us get travel insurance when we take trips. But there's much about insurance that usually goes overlooked.

When you bought your car, for instance, did you agree to credit insurance to pay off the loan? If you did, who was protected—you or the lender? Did you ask about GAP insurance on your leased automobile? Buying and driving an automobile, truck, or motorcycle will require you to obtain the appropriate property and casualty insurance coverage—do you know what that entails? Purchasing and financing a house also will require the appropriate insurance to be purchased—will you want to retire the mortgage if you die prematurely?

Questions abound about insurance coverage, and not just about what kind of insurance you should have. How you go about getting insurance can be as tricky as what kind of insurance you choose to buy. For instance, do you buy your insurance online, in person, directly with the insurance company, or through an agent? Will you work with an independent agent or a company agent? An independent agent offers the opportunity to shop for prices from more than one company. A company agent usually represents one insurance company for auto, home, and life insurance. Regardless of which way you choose to buy, the purchase should be made with a professional agent who is responsive to your needs and knowledgeable about your options.

Another consideration when buying insurance is "bundling" of coverage, which can help lower overall premiums. Multi-car discounts, for example, make it attractive to package auto and home insurance together for a reduced premium as compared to buying separate policies on your house and each car in your garage.

Other coverage, such as disability income protection, life insurance, and health insurance typically do not offer correspondingly similar benefits of bundling, but that doesn't mean you shouldn't consider buying some or all of this coverage.

Disability income insurance, for example, is designed to provide for a partial replacement of salary or wages when the insured is unable to work due to accident or illness. Oftentimes, the typical payment is about 60 to 70 percent of the insured's monthly income. The disability insurance monthly benefits can either be taxable or tax free, depending on who is paying the premium. If you are paying the premiums, the monthly benefit will come to you tax free; but if your employer is paying the premiums, the benefits are taxable.

Disability insurance has a waiting period before benefits are paid out, much like the deductible on auto/home insurance. The waiting period, or "elimination period" as it is sometimes known, differs from policy to policy as an option elected at the time of application. A longer waiting or elimination period, as with a higher deductible, will reduce the premium paid by or on behalf of the insured. Other factors that determine the premium are the length of time a benefit is paid, and the occupation and health history of the applicant.

Young families face a number of obstacles that might prevent them from focusing on insurance and, perhaps, other important aspects of financial planning. Newlyweds and young couples beginning their families encounter many financial distractions that can dissuade them from learning about the steps they should take to protect their financial futures. Although it can be easy to put it off, some attention must be paid to the necessities of risk management, which is the purpose of insurance. An array of insurance decisions must be made throughout the course of your life, and a confusing—and crucial—one for many of us is the purchase of life insurance. There is an abundance of misconceptions regarding the purchase of life insurance. Among the most frequently asked questions are "How much do we need?" and "Who should have the coverage?"

Ted and Alice are a young professional couple with a baby on the way who are facing these very questions. Ted's employer provides him with some life insurance and an option to buy more through payroll deduction. Alice has a flat benefit from her employer's health insurance package. The issue of life insurance was not at the top of their to-do list, but it was something they knew they would eventually have to tackle. Since both of them were younger than 30 years old, did not use tobacco in any form, took no prescription medications, had no DUI/OVI offenses (driving or operating a vehicle under the influence), and were within accepted limits for height–weight ratios, it would be easy for them to obtain a quote showing preferred (i.e., the best) rates. Had they not met these criteria, they would have seen higher rates. Tobacco users, for instance, often see rates quoted for two times the rate of nontobacco users.

Along with how much and what kind of life insurance they should get, another consideration was how much income Ted and Alice wanted life insurance to provide if one of them were to die. Ted's annual salary was $65,000, and Alice's was $45,000, so the couple was generating a pretax combined annual salary of $110,000 or about $9,166 per month. How much insurance is appropriate to replace one of these incomes in the event of the premature death of either of them? When trying to figure out how much insurance to purchase, a rule of thumb is to add a zero to the end of the annual salary. So, in this case, Ted should look to a minimum of $650,000, and Alice should look to have $450,000 in life insurance. The premium for Ted's $650,000 death benefit could be as little as $34 a month for a twenty-year term policy. For Alice, the monthly premium could be as low as $18.

Ted and Alice could purchase additional life insurance through their employers, or they could purchase separate policies. Employer-sponsored insurance generally has two significant features: underwriting and affordability. Life insurance purchased at a group rate, for example, would guarantee coverage and might provide some financial relief for someone with a pre-existing health issue. It also can be convenient to buy a policy through work as premiums come directly out of your paycheck and you need not even think about making the payments every month. Group insurance through the company you work for can be a good option for some people, but it comes with the caveat that if you leave that employer, it oftentimes can be more expensive to take the coverage with you than if you were to buy life insurance on your own. If you opt to buy insurance directly through an insurance company, the portability of the coverage isn't an issue because it is yours already: you don't have to worry about what happens with your life insurance if you change jobs because your employer isn't providing the life insurance coverage.

With that in mind, it's important to note that the insurance you might obtain through your employer is typically "term" insurance, which means that the coverage is for a death benefit only and so you cannot expect a return of premium or savings at some point in the future. Plainly stated, with term insurance, the insured must die for the beneficiary to receive the benefit.

Term insurance has no cash value (also known as "surrender value") and is considered the most cost-effective way to obtain coverage. Although term insurance offers no cash savings like some other forms of insurance do, it does boast lower premiums, which can make it a good option for younger, healthier people. Term life insurance is different from permanent insurance and whole life insurance, which are structured to be in effect for your entire life or until the end of the mortality tables, whichever comes first. In other words, if you live into your seventies, eighties, or nineties, the death benefit on permanent or whole life insurance could still be in place. Permanent and whole life insurance policies build up a cash (savings) value, so it is possible to surrender the policy prior to death and take the savings to use on life benefits rather than death benefits (i.e., you can use the money while you're still living rather than passing the money to your beneficiary upon your death).

With term insurance, death benefits are usually paid out as a lump-sum benefit to the named beneficiary upon the demise of the policyholder. There are alternatives, however, such as accelerated death benefits, which allow the policyholder to use the benefits when facing terminal illness. Sometimes, insurance policies are convertible (e.g., term life could be converted to whole life), and so it's important to consider all the options when purchasing life insurance. Regardless of which option you purchase, it is important to note that premiums will vary. There's no one, right way to go about purchasing a life insurance policy—except to buy one, period.

The wrong way to go about insurance is to skip it altogether. You risk catastrophic financial damage if, say, you're involved in a terrible car crash and have no auto insurance, your house burns down and you have no homeowners insurance, or you die prematurely and leave your family with nothing because you had no life insurance.

It can be easy for young people in particular to take a pass on insurance, especially when they're just starting out and are facing so many other expenses on their own for the first time. However, the bigger risk is in skipping insurance and hoping for the best. Insurance policies protect you and your family against financial ruin. Some insurance policies, such as whole life insurance, provide tax-sheltered savings accounts that can, for instance, help fund life after retirement. Using insurance as a way to reduce taxes can also be a great way to build your nest egg. We'll look more at how you can use taxes to your advantage next, in Chapter 7.

Lessons Learned

- Young couples and families should actively consider all insurance options: home and auto, life and disability income, and health and medical.
- Look carefully at insurance policy options, weighing such considerations as age, family status, health and medical issues,

future needs, and so forth. Insurance policies can be used in any number of ways to protect assets and preserve legacies.

- When considering life insurance, weigh the options—term, permanent, and whole life—against such needs as paying off a mortgage, paying for your children's education, and providing an income for your widow or widower. Choose the policy that will do the most to meet your needs.

CHAPTER 7

Use Taxes to Your Advantage

When you're just starting out in life in the postcollege "real world", getting a new job, living in a new place, maybe even getting married and starting a family, it can be challenging to tackle all the financial tasks that you ought to. It's tough enough juggling student loans, credit card debt, rent, utilities, smartphone bills, and food expenses without having to worry about 401(k) plans, insurance, and taxes.

But you must.

Even though retirement might seem a very, very long way off, it's important to start planning for it, and the sooner the better. As you go through life, it will be important to invest wisely, build a nest egg, establish a rainy day fund, and plan for retirement. You should think about your financial goals and how you want to achieve them.

In fact, there are any number of issues you should consider as you start to lay the foundations for a sound financial future. Where is the best place to invest your money? How much should you be contributing to your 401(k)? Should you put your money into a traditional IRA or a Roth IRA? What about investing in a College Savings 529 Plan? What should be used as an accumulation vehicle for savings?

These are all good questions—and they all need answers. But an often overlooked question relates to Uncle Sam: How can you use taxes to your advantage?

Taxes weigh heavily on our day-to-day finances, savings, and investments, and so tax planning is an integral part of sound financial planning. Because of that, it's important to consider how the taxman views your money. Basically, it boils down to four ways: taxable, tax-deferred, tax-free, and tax-exempt.

Taxable income refers to money you've earned other than through your employer. This income generates a Form 1099, the tax form used for nonemployee compensation, which is sent out annually informing the IRS how much interest, dividend income, or capital gain is being credited to you in a calendar year. This means that banks, brokerage houses, insurance companies, and other financial institutions will report activity on any account associated with your Social Security number. At tax time it will be entered onto your 1040 form, and you then will settle with IRS and the state in which you live. Most of us are familiar with this form of taxation—we've been paying taxes every year we've been working.

Tax-deferred status refers to money on which taxes are paid at a later date. Examples of investment vehicles with tax-deferred status include IRAs, defined-contribution plans, annuities, and life insurance policies. None of these send out 1099s unless there has been a distribution.

Deferring income is most frequently associated with pretax payroll savings plans such as 401(k), 403(b), and 457 plans. The idea is to set aside some money and not pay taxes on it until you retire. The advantages of such defined-contribution plans include the fact that $1 put into your 401(k) does not reduce your take-home pay by $1 but by the net of your tax bracket: if you're in the 15 percent bracket, it costs only 85 cents to save $1. Investing in such tax-deferred plans presumes your budget allows for the deferral of current income, but most people barely notice the money being deposited into this long-term investment.

The strategic use of tax deferral can also be applied to earnings on savings and investments that you prefer not to be taxed at current rates. In this case, the tax code favors the use of insurance company products to achieve the deferral of ordinary (taxable) income. In the most basic of applications, taxable interest-earning instruments can be transferred into a deferred annuity. The interest earned does not generate a 1099 at tax time, and you keep the incidental earnings from being reported until you withdraw them from the annuity contract.

As of this writing, a three-year fixed annuity earns about 2 percent on deposits. Every $100,000 sitting in an annuity contract paying 2 percent earns $2,000 yearly that is not reported to the IRS. Let's say that at the end of the three-year period, you choose to spend money from the annuity. Interest is distributed first and is fully reportable. It is subject to being included in your income for the year of withdrawal and will be taxed at your highest marginal tax bracket. The principal is not reported as taxable provided that after-tax dollars were used to purchase the annuity. The benefit is in keeping incidental ordinary income such as interest from being reported, especially if you would prefer to control when you report earnings on your savings and investments.

Annuities issued by life insurance companies are not the only mechanism available to defer income from being reported. Life insurance contracts are another readily available instrument for use. The differences between life insurance and annuities are found in the underwriting and issue limits. Typically, the only underwriting necessary on a deferred annuity is the validity of the check—if the check clears, the underwriting is done. The exception is an annuity considered for use in paying for long-term care expenses under the guidelines of the Pension Protection Act of 2006, for which there will be some health underwriting.

Life insurance, on the other hand, will require health underwriting whether the policy is for regular scheduled premiums or a single lump-sum premium. The IRS also places restrictions related to the amount of the premium and the face amount (the death benefit) of the policy. These restrictions refer to a classification of insurance policies as modified endowment contracts (MECs) as defined by the 1988 Technical and Miscellaneous Revenue Act (TAMRA). If a policy violates the MEC rule within TAMRA, then distributions from the policy will be treated the same as distributions from an annuity (i.e., they will be taxable) and incur a 10 percent penalty.

Regardless, life insurance under current law continues to allow the accrual of interest earnings to remain free from income tax reporting. One of the sought-after features is the fact that proceeds from an insurance policy in the form of the death benefit remain tax-free to the recipient (corporate-owned life insurance might not be, however). Since death proceeds are income tax free, the other benefit is that withdrawals from non-MEC policies in the form of a loan are tax-free. Loans by definition are not includable income, and this is true for life policy loans.

A final advantage for annuities and life insurance involves the opportunity for high-income individuals to avoid the 3.8 percent Medicare surcharge tax imposed as a result of the Affordable Care Act of 2010. This Medicare surtax is imposed on net investment income in excess of $250,000. Net investment income includes interest, capital gains, rental income, and royalties, among other things.

Tax-free income means either that there is no reporting of the income or that if it is reported, it still isn't taxed. Tax-free income is that income which does not exceed your standard deduction or itemized deductions on your 1040, plus your personal exemptions, plus distributions from Roth IRA accounts if held for the proper amount of time, plus loans from life insurance policies not subject to MEC limitations imposed by TAMRA.

This is not to be confused with tax-exempt interest earned on, for example, municipal bonds or municipal bond funds. Bonds generally exempt from being taxed at the federal level are those issued to finance the construction of roads, sewers, hospitals, or schools, or those issued to allow those same entities to operate. For example, an Ohio bond issued for a project in Ohio and held by an Ohio resident taxpayer will most likely be exempt from both federal and Ohio taxes.

Also relating to tax-exempt income is Social Security. Tax-exempt does not mean that such income isn't included in the issue of determining the amount of Social Security benefits to be added to your taxable income. As of 1984, Social Security benefits are included in gross income for determining federal income taxes. The calculation adds either 50 percent of the Social Security benefits or 85 percent of Social Security benefits to the total gross income, depending on income and filing status.

Tax-exempt interest is not taxed, but the amount received in tax-exempt interest is part of the calculation for determining tax on

Social Security benefits. The interest earned on tax-exempt issues is used to determine the extent to which your Social Security benefits will be taxed. Social Security benefits are subject to being taxed, and that means the tax-exempt income is now provisional income for the purposes of determining how much of the Social Security benefit is taxed.

Tax-exempt interest is more appealing than taxable interest, but the true test requires comparing taxable income to tax-exempt income after applying the impact of your marginal tax bracket. For example, let's say you're considering an investment in a taxable bond mutual fund that yields a 4.5 percent dividend as well as a tax-exempt bond mutual fund yielding 3.5 percent for someone in the 28 percent marginal tax bracket. Which one nets the higher yield?

To determine yield, multiply 4.5 percent by your after-tax net, calculated as 100 percent – 28 percent = 72 percent. The arithmetic shows that 0.045 × 0.72 equals 0.0324 or 3.24 percent. So for those whose highest marginal rate is 28 percent, a yield of 3.5 percent tax exempt on the municipal bond fund is better than the 3.24 percent yield on the taxable bond fund.

Another consideration is whether tax-exempt earnings might keep all of your otherwise ordinary income below the next higher bracket. For example, in 2015 taxable income of $74,899 or below is taxed at 15 percent; income of $74,900 and above is taxed at 25 percent. Let's say you're looking at investing $100,000 from a certificate of deposit which has matured. An online bank is promoting an interest rate of 3 percent for one year. That would produce $3,000 of totally taxable income ($100,000 × 0.03 = $3,000). You like the idea of FDIC insurance and stability of principal; but the interest on income of more than $74,900 is taxed at the higher rate of 25 percent, and will cost you $750 in taxes ($3,000 × 0.25 = $750). Instead, you might consider investing in a tax-exempt fund that pays 2.5 percent, which means you would get to keep the $2,500 tax-free income ($100,000 × 0.025 = $2,500). Remember that the marginal brackets affect the last dollar taxed, so it might be worth the investigation into tax-exempt interest income.

Taxes are a certainty, and you'll face them your entire life. But by knowing and understanding how taxes affect your investments, preretirement income, and distribution of retirement income, you'll be better positioned to plan for and achieve your financial goals, no matter what comes—because sometimes we're beset with unexpected situations that can shake us to our core. One of those, divorce, can have especially painful financial implications. We'll look at that next, in Chapter 8.

Lessons Learned

- When it comes to how your money is taxed, it's important to understand the four basic tax categories: taxable, tax-deferred, tax-free, and tax-exempt.
- Tax-deferred investment vehicles such as IRAs, defined-contribution plans, annuities, and life insurance policies can save thousands of dollars over the life of your financial portfolio.
- Tax-exempt earnings might help you keep all of your otherwise ordinary income below the next higher bracket because the marginal brackets affect the last dollar taxed, so it can be worthwhile to consider tax-exempt income opportunities.

CHAPTER 8

Plan for Change

Human nature makes it difficult to handle change at times. This tendency can get us in financial trouble when it prevents us from making a change that we know that could be beneficial or even necessary.

When making a change, we hope things will improve; but we also know that, unfortunately, things could get worse. The fear of making things worse can freeze us into indecision. This phenomenon is called "status quo bias," and it is ingrained into our subconscious. That's why making changes can be so difficult: we're fighting our subconscious tendency to resist change unless it is clearly beneficial. Status quo bias leads most people to prefer that things remain the same, or if there must be change, that it disrupts as little as possible.

Change also is difficult because we tend to overestimate the value of what we already have and underestimate the value of what we have to gain. When you combine all these psychological factors together, is it any wonder why achieving change is so difficult?

Among the most difficult changes in life is divorce. Tammy, a 42-year-old stay-at-home mom found this out firsthand. Stuck in a miserable marriage with seemingly no way out, she had to face change square in the face.

Tammy was in her early twenties when she married her high school sweetheart, Jason. They had their first child shortly thereafter, and they now have three adorable daughters ranging in ages from 3 to 9.

Their marriage started out fine. Jason had always been a bit arrogant and pushy, but it was nothing Tammy couldn't handle. All their friends liked him, and he was usually the life of the party. But as time went by, things started to change.

Even though Jason was making a good living as a successful real estate broker, their finances became tighter as their young family grew. Jason became more easily agitated, and his temper would flare up much more frequently. He also became more aggressive, condescending, and arrogant. He took particular pleasure in belittling his wife in front of others. His behavior was even worse at home, and he frequently was verbally abusive to Tammy in front of their daughters. As Jason's outbursts got progressively worse, the family situation continued to deteriorate.

Things got so bad that Tammy finally met with a financial advisor to discuss getting a divorce. She explained how horrible her life was with her husband, and how it wasn't fair to their children. She simply couldn't imagine spending the rest of her life like this. Tammy was angry and fed up, and she ultimately decided that she was going to divorce Jason.

Tammy considered her options and imagined what her new life might look like, including her job options, other sources of potential income, and housing arrangements. It was at this point she begin to hesitate.

Once the realization began to set in that her life would change dramatically, Tammy's whole demeanor shifted. She confessed how scary the prospect of divorce—and embarking on a new life—was for her. She had never been alone in her entire life. How would she be able to support her daughters? How would she find time to work and take care of them? The thought of raising three children on her own was simply too overwhelming for her. Tammy soon convinced herself that her situation "maybe really wasn't that bad after all" and that maybe she had made a mistake even thinking about it.

Divorce can be a scary prospect. If not handled well, it even can lead to the financial ruin of a family. In some cases, a couple may already be struggling financially, living paycheck to paycheck with little in savings to fall back on in the event of an emergency. In these instances, no one comes out the winner in a divorce.

In a divorce, income and assets have to be split, leaving both parties with less to live on then they had while they were together, and their expenses will be higher due to having to maintain two households. This reduction in income and increase in expenses will likely take a toll on the lifestyles of both parties.

The situation can be made even worse in a highly contentious divorce. It is not uncommon for a divorce to cost many thousands of dollars. In fact, the average cost of a contested divorce ranges from about $10,000 to $30,000.[9] In those cases, the legal costs further reduce the amount that each party will walk away with, leaving them even worse off financially.

A potential solution is to try divorce mediation first. Divorce mediation can cost much less (about $3,000 to $6,000)[10] than working with attorneys and going to court in a contested divorce. In this process, a divorce mediator will sit down together with both parties to see if a fair and equitable compromise can be reached. This less confrontational setting allows both parties to negotiate on a less emotional level. Not only can divorce mediation be significantly less expensive, but it also can help the parties to separate on more amicable terms. This can be especially beneficial when younger children are involved.

Another factor to consider when negotiating a divorce settlement are the assets involved. Not all assets are equal, even if the values are. For example, a $100,000 IRA or 401(k) account may not net the same amount as a $100,000 savings account. If you took money out of the bank account, you would not owe any taxes; if, however, you took money out of the IRA or 401(k), you would owe taxes and possibly an additional 10 percent in penalties if you were under the age of 59½ at the time of the withdrawal. So in this case, depending on your age and tax bracket, if you needed to take the money out of the account, you could end up with significantly less money than you expected. You may

---

[9]   Lisa Magloff, "The Average Cost for Divorce," *LegalZoom*, 2013. Retrieved August 24, 2015, from http://info.legalzoom.com/average-cost-divorce-20103.html.

[10]   Mediation Matters, "The Cost of Divorce: Three Processes," *Mediation Matters*, n.d. Retrieved August 25, 2015, from http://www.mediationmatters.com/the_cost_of_divorce.php.

have been better off receiving the savings account instead of the IRA or 401(k).

Another mistake when divorcing can be insisting on getting the house, especially if there is still an existing mortgage. You may end up getting the house, but you may owe some amount to your ex-spouse to buy out their portion. This would leave you with the house, but you would have much less in liquid assets.

A common problem occurs when the person who gets the house finds out that keeping it on the reduced income they have coming in after the divorce isn't affordable. If they are forced to sell the house, the net amount they receive after all the expenses are paid (closing costs, real estate commissions, etc.) might be considerably less than what their spouse received in cash. It might have been better to negotiate that the house be sold and the proceeds and expenses split between both parties.

A third common mistake when splitting assets in a divorce concerns pensions and retirement accounts. Significant mistakes can be made when attempting to value retirement benefits, leading to one of the parties being shortchanged. Establishing the present value of a future lifetime pension benefit can be very complicated, and the person doing the calculations should have a good understanding of both finances and pension benefits. Whether using a divorce attorney or mediator, it is crucial to establish a fair value of pensions and retirement accounts.

Per The National Marriage Project, University of Virginia 2012, the divorce rate in the United States hovers around 45 percent for first marriages and is even higher for subsequent marriages. The average age of couples going through their first divorce is 30 years old. No matter what age you might be when contemplating divorce, it's important to consider the financial implications, which include what your new budget will look like, how best to divvy up financial assets, what to do with the house, and how to pay for the cost of the divorce itself.

It can be helpful to work with a financial advisor well before hiring a divorce attorney so that you can get a better handle on the assets such as the balances in the checking and savings accounts as well as the decisions to be made such as how much emergency cash to set aside and what to do with credit cards. Divorce will affect everything from your bank accounts to your insurance policies to your will and estate plans, so it's important to consider the financial implications and how they will affect you.

Lessons Learned

- Divorce can come at a high cost. The legal procedure itself can cost as much as $30,000. The parties involved will also have to learn how to finance two households instead of one, which can negatively affect family budgets and savings.
- Splitting assets in a divorce should be done carefully—and as objectively as possible. For example, although the impulse for most people is to fight to keep the house, it's important to consider the actual costs of such assets and liabilities over the long haul.
- Those who plan to divorce should be sure to calculate the present value of a future lifetime pension benefit and other retirement accounts so that one party isn't shortchanged.

Part II

Build Your Savings as You Plan for the Future

You buy a home, you raise your family, you earn some promotions, maybe you even enter into a new relationship or a second marriage. A lot can happen in life, whether or not you're planning for the milestones that make our memories.

It's during these years that we move beyond so many firsts—our first apartments, our first car, our first child—and we look toward the future to start building our lives and our nest eggs. It's during these years that we start thinking not just about saving and investing but also about preparing for the future with life insurance, healthcare planning, and estate planning. The future is coming faster than you might like to think—and so is the need to plan for it.

CHAPTER 9

Prepare for Rainy Days

The power of the consumer-driven culture in America can sometimes seem overwhelming. Contemporary values and goals lead people to aspire to a lifestyle at least equal to or better than that of their neighbors, or even one that matches some sort of ideal fantasy promoted by the media and popular culture. As a result, many families wind up having their personal identities tied to acquiring and owning a wide array of material possessions, which can sometimes lead to disastrous consequences.

Such was the case with Phil and Irene. Phil was a corporate manager in his middle fifties who had worked for decades for a blue-chip company. He was enjoying a comfortable salary in the $200,000 range along with generous health insurance and retirement benefits. Irene was a stay-at-home mom who had focused on raising their children, who were now all grown up and out of school. Phil and Irene were living the American dream, but in doing so they hadn't realized how their spending patterns had become increasingly lavish and out of control. It all came to a screeching halt one day when Phil was called into his boss's office and told that he was being laid off as part of a corporate restructuring. On that very day, their lives were changed forever.

Phil and Irene took a few days to digest the news. Then, for the first time in many years, they started to take a serious look at their financial situation to determine what their options were. The more they scrutinized their situation, the uglier it looked.

The couple first needed to examine their cash reserves, money that's readily available to pay living expenses, immune from market ups and downs, and accessible without any significant fees or costs. Cash reserves include money in bank accounts such as savings and checking accounts, credit union accounts, certificates of deposit, and U.S. savings bonds. The starting point for every family's financial security is to have an adequate level of cash reserves, sometimes called a "rainy day fund."

The actual level of cash reserves that a family should have depends on a variety of factors. A good starting point for most people is to maintain a fund equal to about three to six months of living expenses. In some cases, this may be enough. If your job is relatively secure and your income is consistent, as for example with some types of government jobs, you might get by with less. In other cases, if you have an unstable job and/or variable income, such as with sales jobs that mostly pay commissions or big bonuses that are highly dependent on company profitability, you might need more. Another factor to consider is the number of income streams coming into the household; households with two incomes might need lower cash reserves, while those depending on just one income might need more.

Also important to determining cash reserve amounts is the level of debt in the household. Those who have a lot of debt would need more, while those who have paid off their houses and cars, for example, and don't have any other debt might need less. One other important factor is that households with a lot of dependents typically need more cash reserves, while those with fewer people (for example, if the children are grown and gone) tend to need less.

Phil and Irene had never contemplated the possibility of Phil losing the job that they had both taken for granted for so many years. They were actually very fortunate that Phil was given six months' salary as part of his severance package (many people in today's economy wouldn't have that luxury), but after taxes were taken out, that only amounted to about $70,000. They were shocked to realize that other than that, they only had about $3,000 in additional cash reserves. In other words, they had basically been living a lifestyle with zero cash reserves. Nor was there anything else in any deposit accounts, no investments, no mutual funds ... nothing. When they added up their monthly living expenses, it became clear that the severance money would last only about six months.

Certainly many families could make $70,000 last for much longer than six months, but Phil's and Irene's balance sheet revealed other, more serious problems. They owed a total of about $85,000 on about ten different credit cards from a whole assortment of issuers, including banks and a variety of retailers. The average interest rate was about 18 percent, which means that they were paying about $15,000 a year just in interest. This was a major reason why their monthly living expenses were so high, and why the severance money wasn't going to last very long.

There could be many reasons for carrying such a high balance on credit cards, such as an extended illness that was not covered by health insurance, a divorce, a significant interruption in income over the years, or some other family emergency. When attempting to explain their debt, Phil and Irene just looked at each other and shook their heads: There was no smoking gun. They had been married for many years, his employment had been steady for decades, and nothing remarkable had happened. The simple fact is that they had just never sat down together and added up all the credit card balances. It had taken this crisis for them to come to the realization that, despite Phil's generous salary, they had been living beyond their means and had been using credit cards to spend more than they earned each year.

This is all too common in American households. As we discussed in Chapter 2, far too many people don't understand how credit cards should really be used. The most responsible way to use credit cards is to think of them strictly as an alternative to carrying a big wad of cash in your pocket, and to use them only to the extent that you can pay the entire balance every month. In this way, you will avoid paying interest, which can have a devastating effect on your overall financial health. Credit card companies make hefty profits on the interest they charge, which is why they often do everything they can to encourage consumers to run up big balances and make just the minimum payments. Most consumers are completely unaware that if the credit card charges 15 to 20 percent interest, the minimum payment is often structured such that the borrower will wind up paying interest equal to two or three times the principal balance over the life of the loan. It's all too easy for this deceptive fact to be covered up by what appears to be a low minimum monthly payment.

The single biggest sign that you're abusing credit cards is if you're not paying off the balance completely every month. Other signs could include relying on them as your only source of cash reserves, having credit cards from every store where you shop, and/or constantly playing the shell game of transferring the balance from one card to another.

In situations in which borrowers like Phil and Irene are suddenly hit with a financial crisis, one little known tactic is to negotiate with the credit card issuers. In many cases, the issuer would rather take a settlement offer for a portion of the total balance and forgive the rest rather than face complete default by a borrower. But this is not a perfect solution; issuers are usually unwilling to discuss such settlements until a borrower has already missed a lot of payments. As a result, the borrowers in these cases may still wind up with damaged credit ratings. In the case of Phil and Irene, they couldn't even consider this option because they didn't have the money with which to make a settlement offer in the first place.

They couldn't use the money from Phil's severance package because they had to conserve their cash reserves for an even more important priority: their monthly mortgage and home equity loan payments. As it turns out, they also hadn't been paying attention to their home equity loan balance, and had been using that loan to fund their lifestyle, just like they were doing with their credit cards. As a result, their total balance owed between their mortgage and their home equity loan was equal to about 95 percent of the value of their home. This meant two things, neither of them good. First of all, they would have to focus all their cash reserves on making those monthly payments so that they wouldn't lose their home. Since credit card debt is usually unsecured, defaulting on those loans will hurt your credit rating, but at least that won't put you out of your home. On the other hand, defaulting on debt that is secured by your home will eventually result in eviction. Second, the high balances on their mortgage and home equity loan also made it less practical to consider the option of selling their home and moving to a less expensive place to live, since they would be left with nothing to put down on a smaller home or even a security deposit to place on an apartment.

Amazingly, Phil's and Irene's debt problems didn't end there. They also had a total of five loans on various vehicles: one car for each of them, two additional cars for their eldest son and their daughter, and an all-terrain vehicle for their youngest son. This is a common issue with many parents: even after the children are educated and grown up, the parents continue to fund a portion of their children's lifestyle. In the case of Phil and Irene, funding the car loans had allowed their daughter to take a lower-paying job and still live in an expensive downtown apartment in a big city where she enjoyed a plethora of entertainment and lifestyle amenities with her circle of friends. It also had allowed their adult son to work only part time while living at home with them and ride the ATV in his spare time. Many parents find it difficult to "cut the financial cord" with their adult children, which can compound problems when they run into their own financial issues themselves.

Believe it or not, yet another issue became evident. Phil had been fortunate enough to be employed for many years at a blue-chip manufacturing company that had a 401(k) plan with a generous employer matching contribution. For most employees in today's economy, this is not the case; employers are not required to make any matching contribution at all into 401(k) plans and many don't. For those that do, the matching contribution is usually very low, often no more than 3 percent of the employee's salary. That's why it's so important for employees to defer as much of their salary as possible into their 401(k) plans.

In previous generations, employees could often rely on fixed pension plans (known as "defined-benefit plans") to provide a steady monthly stream of income at retirement. Combined with Social Security, this often was enough to afford a comfortable retirement lifestyle for employees. But in recent decades, employers are increasingly turning away from defined-benefit plans, which are expensive for them to maintain. Instead, employers are turning to 401(k) plans, which are funded mostly by employee salary deferrals. This is a much cheaper arrangement for employers.

The result is that we are in the midst of nothing less than a retirement revolution, a fundamental transformation where the future picture of retirement will be very different, characterized by workers having nothing but their 401(k)s to rely on, along with Social Security. In a sense, this is a sort of grand social experiment because 401(k) plans are different from defined-benefit fixed pension plans in so many ways. With defined-benefit plans, all the responsibility is with the employer. It's up to the employer to calculate the employee's benefit, keep them informed as to the amount of expected retirement income, and, most important, to fund the plan and manage the investments every year so that there is enough money to pay the promised benefits.

But with 401(k) and other defined-contribution plans, the roles are almost entirely reversed. With 401(k) plans, it's up to the employee to make all the decisions. It's the employee who decides whether to participate in the first place, what percentage of their salary to contribute, and which investments to use among those offered by the plan. This is a lot of responsibility, and it remains to be seen whether most employees are up to the task of making sound decisions about these matters. As just one example, employees who are going to have to rely primarily on their 401(k) plan for retirement income should generally contribute at least 10 percent of their salary each year, but many fall far short of that figure.

In Phil's case, the employer had been making a relatively generous 6 percent matching contribution to his 401(k), resulting in a balance of $400,000 in his account. But there was a problem. Consistent with his other poor financial habits, Phil had borrowed $75,000 from his 401(k) plan, and so his statement showed an outstanding loan balance in that amount.

This created two different problems for Phil. The first is that it's generally a bad principle for an employee to borrow from a 401(k) plan: he is robbing himself of one of the most valuable assets he has, time. Time is required for the tried and true method of building wealth that involves putting as much money away as soon possible and letting the miracle of compound interest work its magic. If you drain your 401(k) balance by borrowing from it and then taking years to put the money back, you're losing out on all those years of compound interest, years you can never have back. The result will be a much smaller 401(k) balance than would otherwise have been the case. That's why a 401(k) plan should be looked upon exclusively as a vehicle to build retirement income, and not as a piggy bank to fund current living expenses, which is what Phil had been doing.

Another potentially even more insidious problem with borrowing from a 401(k) plan arises from the little-known rule that if your employment is terminated for any reason, you generally have to repay any 401(k) loan balances in full, typically within two months. If the employee doesn't do that, the entire loan balance is treated as a distribution, which means that it becomes taxable income, subject to a 10 percent penalty if the employee is under age 59½.

Obviously this can be a huge problem in cases where the employee is unexpectedly terminated in a situation like a layoff, when he may be in no position to repay the loan, which is exactly what happened to Phil. Being short on cash reserves, Phil couldn't repay the loan and so had to endure a painful tax bill just when he could least afford to do so.

At this point, Phil's and Irene's options were extremely limited. They didn't have the cash reserves to repay the 401(k) loan and so had to pay the resulting income tax and penalty. They didn't have the cash to make any settlement offers on their credit card debts and so had to make difficult choices about whether to make those heavy monthly payments or default on them (which would hurt their credit) in order to conserve cash and make the mortgage and home equity loan payments for a little while longer. They had to decide whether to make their children unexpectedly start paying for their own vehicle loans, something the eldest daughter would not be able to do without moving to a less expensive apartment, which would entail a much longer commute. Furthermore, they couldn't consider filing bankruptcy for many months, since Phil's severance income disqualified him from that option for the time being.

Ultimately, Phil was able to find another good job, but it took about three years. In the meantime, he wound up taking some temporary jobs, which he hated and which caused him so much stress that he developed stomach trouble and some depression. In order to stay in his home during that three-year period, he resorted to spending down more than half of his 401(k) plan, which was his only retirement asset. Since he was in his early sixties by that time, he will never have time to recoup the hit to his 401(k) plan. As a result, his retirement will be permanently affected.

There are many lessons to be learned from what happened to Phil and Irene. No one should make financial decisions as if one's job will last forever. It's critically important to have an adequate level of cash reserves at all times. Debt should be carefully managed, and credit card balances should always be paid off each month. In addition, 401(k) plans should be used exclusively as a vehicle for future retirement income, with loans taken against them only in the case of emergency (and an emergency doesn't mean, for example, that the entire house must be redecorated in time for Thanksgiving).

Managing debt and credit, building savings, and contributing to 401(k) plans are important when it comes to covering the expenses of daily life while investing for the future. It's important to plan as early as possible for the future you want, and to revisit that plan frequently. We'll look at that next, in Chapter 10.

Lessons Learned

- A crucial part of any financial plan is to establish enough cash reserves (i.e., your rainy day fund) to help you face any unexpected events that might diminish your income. How much you need varies, but most people set aside three to six months' of income in an easily accessible account.
- Credit cards, home equity loans, and 401(k) plans should never be used like cash to fund everyday living expenses or to keep you in a comfortable lifestyle. Debt should be paid off right away in order to avoid building up high balances with huge interest rates that make it impossible to keep up payments.
- Parents should be wary of funding their children's lifestyles once they've grown and left the coop, as it were. Talk to your children about cutting the financial cord so that they can become financially independent and so that you can save more money for your own retirement.

CHAPTER 10

Plan Early and Often

Once upon a time, Americans used personal savings for extras such as vacations, a new car, or entertainment, putting few expenses on credit cards and taking out loans only when necessary. Those were the days when Americans depended primarily on their pensions and Social Security benefits to cover their retirement expenses. These individuals worked most of their careers at one company, earning a valuable pension that paid them a guaranteed income, complementing their Social Security benefits. However, this has changed rather dramatically over the past three decades or so.

According to the U.S. Department of Labor, in 1979, 62 percent of employees' retirement plans included a pension, yet in 2011, only 7 percent of employees' retirement plans included a pension. Though Social Security was, and still is, the main source of retirement income, the Voya Retire Ready Index study recently found that 58 percent of respondents were significantly concerned that they would end up with fewer Social Security benefits than currently projected by the Social Security Administration.

The trends toward the elimination of pension funds and the possibility of lower Social Security benefits clearly place more emphasis than ever on personal savings. As a result, one might expect Americans to respond by saving more for their retirement. Yet, they actually aren't responding in this manner.

How much money each individual needs to save in order to support a comfortable retirement depends on many factors, including age, marital status, Social Security benefits, pension income, annuity income, and any other guaranteed income sources. It also is extremely dependent on how much the individual or couple expects to spend in retirement. Savings will fund the difference between guaranteed income sources and retirement expenses. How those savings are invested, and the resulting earnings over time, will have a material impact on the success of a retirement plan. Everyone has different needs, and Mary and John serve as a good example of a plan that worked well for a comfortable retirement.

Mary and John started dating in high school. They went off to separate colleges, but reunited after graduation and soon married. They both had good jobs and bought their first home a few years later. The following year, they started a family and made the decision to hire a nanny so Mary could go back to work. Two years later, Mary was pregnant again and they had another child.

Financial security was important to Mary and John, and they were doing everything right. When they first got married, they met with a financial planner. They had a lot of questions about when they should start saving to buy a house, when to put money away for college expenses for children, whether they needed life insurance, when they needed to start saving for retirement, and whether they needed to worry about saving for long-term care insurance. They wanted to know whether it was better to save for retirement using their employer's 401(k) plan or to just put money in a savings account.

One of their financial planner's first recommendations was to contribute to their employer's 401(k) plan, investing 70 percent in stocks and 30 percent in fixed income securities. Because they were young, they had plenty of time to ride out the short-term volatility of the stock market in order to capture its historical long-term gains. Of course, past results are no guarantee of future results, so Mary and John invested accordingly and continued to monitor their portfolio to see if they needed to reallocate based on their needs and market conditions.

The couple continued to have success in their careers, and so they both increased the contributions to their 401(k) plans each year. Both of their employers matched a percentage of their contributions, up to a certain limit, further enhancing the growth in their account balances. John's employer matched 50 percent up to the first 5 percent of his income, and Mary's employer matched 100 percent of the first 4 percent and then 50 percent of the next 2 percent of her income. The result was that if John contributed at least 5 percent, then the employer deposited another 2.5 percent into his 401(k) account, for a total of 7.5 percent. If Mary contributed at least 6 percent, then the employer contributed another 5 percent, for a total of 11 percent.

Mary and John's strategy was consistent with the results of a survey by the Employee Benefit Research Institute and Greenwald and Associates. The survey found that contributing to an employer-sponsored retirement plan, such as a 401(k) or 403(b), was one of the key factors in successful retirement planning. They reported that 44 percent of people without an employer-sponsored retirement plan were unsure whether they would have enough money saved for retirement versus only 14 percent of those with such a retirement plan. In other words, while they may or may not be saving the right amount, 86 percent of those who are contributing to an employer-sponsored retirement plan felt better about their retirement savings.

In addition to investing in their 401(k) plans, Mary and John purchased guaranteed term life insurance policies to protect their earning years while their children grew up. They selected an amount that provided each of them with enough money to carry on without the other spouse in the event of a premature death. Along the way, they also purchased a small amount of long-term care insurance to offset some of the expenses in the event that either of them contracted a severe illness at some point in the future.

As the kids grew up, they set aside funds to help pay for college expenses. They also helped pay for two weddings. In the meantime, Mary and John continued to have success in their careers, eventually moving into middle management with their respective employers. They also developed a retirement plan when they got into their fifties in order to be sure that they were on track to retire in their sixties. They defined their retirement goals and set up specific saving goals that would support their desired retirement lifestyle.

A major factor affecting retirement planning is longevity. Americans are living longer, healthier, and more active lives in retirement. The average life expectancy of a 65-year-old is now 84 years, according to a report issued in October 2014 by the National Center for Health Statistics. For comparison, a 65-year-old in 2000 was expected to live until age 83, up from 81 in 1980, 79 in 1960, and 78 in 1940.

This is good news for those who want to have a long retirement. But it also means that you may need to save more money for your retirement plan. If you worked from age 22 to age 65, you earned an income for 43 years. This income allowed you to live your life, possibly buy a house or a car, or take vacations when you wanted to. It also allowed you to potentially raise a family and send your kids to college or help them buy their first house (or both).

Of course, that income vanishes when you retire and are no longer drawing a paycheck from an employer. Then you also are no longer contributing toward your retirement savings account or getting a match of your 401(k) contributions from your employer. You're on your own. So what does that mean? It means that you have to balance your lifetime savings against your retirement expenses.

Mary and John both retired when they reached age 65. They were healthy and ready to live an active retirement. They signed up for Medicare, and each of them rolled their 401(k) into an IRA. They updated their overall retirement plan, taking into consideration each of their projected Social Security benefits and current savings and adjusting it for any changes in their retirement goals. They were now grandparents, and the kids had settled in two separate cities, so they included additional travel expenses.

Mary and John were smart to begin early with their financial planning, not only looking at simple budgeting and establishing a rainy day fund, but also investing for their future and their children's futures. As it happens, however, they were exceptions to the rule when compared to most Americans. In a recent survey, the Employee Benefit Research Institute and Greenwald and Associates found these numbers:

- 64 percent of respondents admit that they are behind schedule when it comes to planning and saving for retirement; only 48 percent have even tried to calculate how much they will need to have saved by the time they retire so they can live comfortably.

- 35 percent of workers who have an employer-sponsored retirement plansay that they have saved at least $100,000 for retirement; only 3 percent of those without a plan have that much money saved.
- 40 percent of workers say that they spent eight hours or more planning for the holidays this past year, while only 34 percent spent that much time planning for retirement.
- 63 percent of retirees say that Social Security provides a major source of income for them.
- 35 percent of retirees have less than $1,000 in savings and investments that could be used for retirement, not counting their primary residence or pensions, and 53 percent have less than $25,000.

These findings are sobering. Americans are clearly not focused on retirement planning. Fortunately, Mary and John made it a priority and started early. Their retirement plan fit them well, and, because they had begun saving when they were young, they were confident that they very likely would have enough savings to support the retirement lifestyle they wanted. The long-term projections seemed realistic, taking taxes and inflation into consideration, along with projected growth of their retirement savings. They adjusted their investment strategy in order to reduce the severity of a stock market correction as they approached retirement, increasing their exposure to fixed income securities and reducing their exposure to equities. They also planned to periodically review their plan in order to confirm that they were still on track and to make adjustments as needed.

Mary and John were lucky that they didn't face any significant issues such as unemployment or major illness prior to retiring. They felt well prepared for retirement and hoped to remain healthy and active, traveling as often as possible to see their children and grandchildren. They even considered moving to one of the cities where their children live to be closer to them, but decided to wait a few years. Life was good!

Couples or individuals who plan ahead like Mary and John typically do well in retirement because they have managed their own expectations. Mary and John were successful in achieving their plan by starting saving early and taking advantage of professional help in projecting the savings required to support their desired lifestyle.

In his book *The 7 Habits of Highly Effective People,* author Stephen Covey advised readers to "begin with the end in mind." It means that if you know where you are going and you acknowledge where you are now, you can take the next step in the right direction to help you better achieve your goals.

Defining financial goals early in life, at least conceptually, provides focus and allows a couple, or individual, to increase the probability of success in retirement planning and other aspects of life. More important, early planning can allow you to live your desired retirement lifestyle for many years to come, which is good because retirement is a big change in your life. It is definitely a paradigm shift. As such, retirement requires a change in focus and discipline. An individual or couple needs to address three major changes:

1. "I don't have a paycheck anymore." Instead of collecting a paycheck, income switches to Social Security payments, pension payments, and/or savings. And, in the future, retirement plans will likely become much more dependent on lifetime savings.
2. "I no longer have a job." As easy as that sounds, some folks have a tough time giving up their day jobs, no longer contributing as they had prior to retiring.
3. "I don't have anything to do." Right behind having a tough time giving up their jobs, many people struggle with what they are going to do in retirement.

The decision to stop working is a tough one. Sometimes, it's a voluntary decision and sometimes it's not. A 2014 Gallup survey found that half of retirees were forced to retire sooner than expected. They also found that most working Americans expect to retire at age 66, up from 63 in 2002. But most Americans don't stay on the job nearly that long. The average retirement age among retirees is now 62, according to Gallup, which is a recent development. The average retirement age hovered around 60 for most of the past decade.

A lot of factors affect when someone stops working and retires— more than we can get into in these pages. Whatever the reason, retirement can be quite stressful. It also can be difficult for someone nearing retirement to figure out what to do after leaving their day job.

No matter the reason or timing, retirement puts pressure on a financial plan. Once retired, the individual or couple becomes completely dependent on retirement income sources. Some are able to live on Social Security and pension income benefits or even just Social Security alone. But those individuals are becoming more the exception than the norm. More and more retirees are dependent on their retirement savings for fixed expenses as well as extra, discretionary items, such as vacations, entertainment, and remodeling. Recent trends suggest that the future burden of retirement income will be increasingly placed on the shoulders of retirement savings.

So, what do you do? Let's look at Carol and Bob. They had met with a financial planner when they were in their early fifties to develop a retirement plan based on certain assumptions that, as they neared retirement, needed to be updated. Bob ultimately retired at age 66, when Carol was age 64. Bob chose to wait until he turned 66 because it was his full retirement age according to Social Security, and he started his Social Security benefits immediately after retiring. Carol had worked most of her life, too, so she qualified for Social Security benefits as well. Although the original plan called for Carol to retire when Bob did, she chose to wait until she turned age 66 before retiring, allowing her to collect her full retirement benefits as well.

Neither Carol nor Bob had a pension. So, beyond Social Security, they had to depend on their savings. Just before Bob retired, they updated their expense budget so that it fit better with their investment strategy and supported the lifestyle they had planned for before they retired. With the help of their financial planner, in preparation for retirement, they had divided their retirement investment plan into three major buckets. The buckets allowed Carol and Bob to combine long-term growth potential with a portion in safer investments for current income. By protecting a portion of the portfolio and eventually setting up monthly withdrawals, they could receive a steady income in addition to their Social Security benefits, providing enough total income to support their projected retirement expenses.

The first bucket was projected to cover Years 1–10 of retirement. It was invested in low-risk, income-producing investments. There was very little expectation for growth from this portion of their portfolio. Because they knew that their short-term income needs would be protected, this strategy allowed them to weather the storm when the more aggressive portions of their portfolio took a downturn.

The second bucket covered Years 11–20 and was invested in a more balanced allocation with a slightly higher growth estimate than the first bucket. This portion would eventually feed the first bucket as the funds in the first bucket were depleted.

The third bucket covered Years 20 until death and was invested in the most aggressive allocation and had the highest growth estimate. This portion would most likely be the most volatile, meaning the balance could go up and down somewhat dramatically. But because the time frame was longer, Bob and Carol felt comfortable with the potential volatility, knowing they wouldn't need the money for years to come.

Determining how much of their retirement savings they needed to put in each bucket was based estimating the expenses associated with each decade and assigning a projected annual return to each portfolio allocation. This strategy was flexible and gave Carol and Bob the confidence to invest some of their portfolio in the more aggressive investments while protecting their short-term income needs.

As expected, market results did vary and they occasionally adjusted their lifestyle in response to those results. Defining a set budget and staying within that budget gave them confidence that their plan would work throughout their retirement. Since the investment results varied from year to year, they found that their asset balance would sometimes exceed their annual goal and sometimes not, but over time, their asset balance stayed in line with their long-term plan.

As they progressed through retirement, their financial planner worked with them to make sure that they had enough liquid assets to support the next five-year increment with minimal market risk.

This portion of the portfolio, invested with asset preservation as the primary goal, was not exposed to the more volatile areas of the various investment options. The rest of their portfolio was designed to provide a certain amount of long-term growth. Unless a retired individual, or couple, is extremely well off, it is critical that a portion of the portfolio is invested in a manner that provides the potential to grow at a pace equal to or faster than the cost of living.

Many of us know that inflation increases the cost of basic expenses. Consider the cost of a McDonald's hamburger. When Ray Kroc sold his first McDonald's hamburger in 1955, it cost 15 cents. By 1975, the cost had doubled to 30 cents. By 1995, the cost had increased to 85 cents. By 2015, the cost had grown to $1.29. Inflation is the reason that the price of a McDonald's hamburger rose from 15 cents to $1.29 today, a 3.65 percent per year increase. Historically, inflation has averaged 3.22 percent from 1913 to 2013, according to InflationData.com, so the price of a McDonald's hamburger has been pretty consistent with inflation. Not that retirees should plan on buying McDonald's hamburgers, but they do need to take inflation into consideration when projecting their retirement expenses.

Carol and Bob were fortunate—and smart. Always frugal, they saved enough during their working years to support their conservative retirement lifestyle expectations. Planning before they retired and continuing the appropriate investment strategies during retirement allowed them to enjoy their golden years. They successfully used savings to supplement their Social Security benefits to cover the fixed expenses and spend on discretionary items as they saw fit.

Of course, not everyone faces the same challenges. While some have defined-contribution plans such as 401(k) or 403(b) plans, some of us still have defined-benefit plans. These pensions also require some planning, and we'll look at that next, in Chapter 11.

Lessons Learned

- As retirement savings continue to shift from defined-benefit plans—pensions—to defined-contribution plans—for example,

401(k) plans—it becomes increasingly important to save more for retirement, in conjunction with an overall financial plan.

- Your savings will make up the difference between sources of guaranteed income, such as Social Security benefits, and expenses you incur during your retirement years. How those savings are invested, and the resulting earnings over time, will have a material impact on the success of your retirement plan.

- It can be helpful to divide your retirement savings and investments into three buckets covering Years 1–10 of your retirement, Years 11–20, and Year 20 and beyond. The assets in each bucket should be carefully allocated in order to meet needs and expenses during your retirement years while keeping pace with inflation and the cost of living.

CHAPTER 11

Pick the Right Pension Plan

Thinking about living your retirement years in thirds (Years 1–10, Years 11–20, and Year 20 and beyond) can be an excellent way to structure your financial plan so you can retire well. No matter what sources of income you plan to live on, it's important to think about how that income will last during the course of your life. There are so many things to think about.

One of the most critical retirement decisions a person has to make is deciding which option to choose from their company's pension plan. The decision could very well determine how a surviving spouse will live out his or her retirement years. It's an important decision with lasting implications, yet most people spend more time deciding what to eat at a restaurant.

Employees who are eligible for a guaranteed monthly pension from their employers need to decide how to take their monthly payments when they're getting ready to retire. Guaranteed pensions ultimately are subject to the company being able to meet its financial obligations. Typically a retiree can choose from a few different monthly retirement benefit options: Single Life, Joint and Survivor, and Period Certain.

The Single Life option will pay a guaranteed monthly benefit that lasts for the entire life of the retiree but, if married, will pay nothing to the surviving spouse. This option will typically pay the highest lifetime monthly benefit. This might be the most practical choice for single retirees, but for someone who is married, careful analysis should be done before deciding on this option, as it might leave the surviving spouse in dire financial straits depending on what other retirement income is available. When choosing this option, the spouse has to sign a waiver acknowledging the fact that he or she understands that no survivor benefits will be distributed. An alternative to picking the Single Life option, which might put the surviving spouse at risk, is to use life insurance to offset the loss of income. We will discuss this further later in the chapter.

Typically, most monthly pensions will offer several Joint and Survivor options. These options pay a lower monthly amount to the retiree, but all or a portion of the monthly benefit will continue for the surviving spouse. (Some pension plans allow the owner to name a nonspousal surviving beneficiary, such as a domestic partner or child.) There are several common continuing survivor benefit options, including 25 percent, 50 percent, 75 percent, or 100 percent of the original amount that the retiree received while living. The higher the percentage left to the surviving spouse, the lower the amount the retiree receives while alive. Table 1 shows an example of how this might work.

Table 1: Typical Joint and Survivor Benefit Options

Benefit Type	Amount Retiree Receives While Alive	Amount Survivor Spouse Receives
Single Life	$1,000/month	$0/month
Joint and Survivor 50 percent	$900/month	$450/month
Joint and Survivor 100 percent	$800/month	$800/month

As you can see, the monthly amount that the retiree receives is decreased depending on how much he or she wishes to leave the spouse. The more left to the surviving spouse, the lower the monthly pension will be while the pension owner is alive.

Some pension plans also offer options that allow a retiree to receive benefits for a certain number of years. These Period Certain options pay benefits for a predetermined period of time, such as ten or twenty years. These options typically pay the highest monthly income, since they are not committed to making monthly payments for the retiree's entire lifetime. If the retiree were to die before the period ends, the remaining payments would be paid out to a designated beneficiary. This is unlike the Single Life benefit that would end at the death of the retiree, even if the retiree died shortly after retiring.

Some plans offer options that combine Single Life and Period Certain options. For example, a pension plan might pay a lifetime benefit, but at least for ten years. That way if the retiree were to die within the first ten years of retirement, it would at least guarantee payments to someone else, so at least ten years' worth of payments were paid out. If the retiree were to die after ten years, no additional payments would be made.

Picking the right option is critical, but, as you can see, it is not necessarily simple. Careful consideration and analysis should be made before deciding on which option to choose. The following are two examples of how important it is to give thoughtful consideration to choosing a pension option.

Frank and Tina had both been previously married, and both had children of their own. They both worked good jobs, but Frank had considerably more assets than his new wife. Tina was ten years younger than Frank and so decided to keep working after he retired. At first it wasn't a problem, but after a year or so, Frank was pressuring Tina to retire as well so they could travel together more.

Frank, being a bit selfish, had chosen the Single Life pension option, which gave him the highest monthly benefit. His rationale was that Tina hadn't even been around when he earned his pension benefits, and so he saw no reason why he should take a reduction in his monthly retirement income. With the Single Only option, Tina would not receive any continuing pension benefits upon Frank's death.

To further complicate the matter, it was Frank's intention to leave the bulk of his assets to his children at his death, and only a smaller amount to Tina. His logic was that Tina's ex-husband was quite well off, and her children would receive a fairly large inheritance from him.

This put Tina in a precarious situation. If Frank were to die first, her retirement income and lifestyle would drop dramatically. So while Tina would have loved to retire and start traveling with Frank, she was afraid that if he died first, she would have to move and make other drastic changes to her lifestyle, since her income would drop significantly. So to help mitigate these risks, she chose to continue to keep working, which didn't make either of them happy.

There was another option, however. Frank could have purchased a life insurance policy and named Tina as the beneficiary. This would have allowed his children to receive the bulk of his assets while still providing enough income to Tina to ensure her financial survival after his death. This would have allowed Frank to still pick the Single Life pension option and use some of the money from the higher monthly payments to pay for the life insurance policy.

Unfortunately, Frank decided that life insurance was simply a waste of money. So Tina continued to work and the resentment continued to fester.

As it turns out, Frank was also shortsighted.

As time went on, the situation got worse. Frank resented the fact that Tina continued to work, and Tina resented the fact that she had to continue to work. Over the next few years, the marriage disintegrated, and Frank filed for divorce.

The irony of the story is that Tina ended up receiving a sizable divorce settlement and retired shortly thereafter. In the long run, the life insurance would have ended up being a lot cheaper for Frank.

Frank and Tina aren't the only ones who have faced such decisions. Knowing when to retire and the manner in which to take a pension can be challenging. Jack and Jenny found this out firsthand.

Jack retired from a large manufacturing company, where he had worked as an assistant plant manager for nearly forty years. Jack's goals had been to retire before he turned age 60 and to make sure that his wife, Jenny, would be taken care of if he were to die first. Jack's concerns were not without merit.

History had shown that the men in Jack's family were not known for longevity. His father, both of his grandfathers, and three of his uncles all died before age 60. As a matter of fact, only two men on both sides of his family lived beyond 60 years of age. And, although Jack took very good care of himself, he wanted to make sure that he had at least a few good years of retirement with his wife.

As Jack closed in on his sixtieth birthday, he requested a meeting with the head of Human Resources at his company. When he met with her, Jack still hadn't decided whether he was quite ready to retire. He liked his job and the people he worked with, but his own life expectancy was still a major concern. He was also worried that if he retired now, he might run out of money in retirement. This was especially a concern to Jenny, so working a few more years would certainly help the situation.

As Jack reviewed his company's retirement options, he discovered a problem: If he were to die before he retired, Jenny would be eligible for only a fraction of his pension. To ensure that Jenny would be taken care of, he had to retire now, whether he wanted to or not.

To make sure that Jenny was protected financially, Jack selected the 100 percent Joint and Survivor pension option. This meant that he would take a 21 percent reduction in his monthly benefits, but it guaranteed that Jenny would continue to get that same amount for the rest of her life as well.

In a cruel turn of events, less than three years after he retired, Jenny suffered a massive heart attack and passed way shortly thereafter. This left Jack continuing to get his reduced pension for the remainder of his life, but with no beneficiary to benefit from it.

Comparing the two couples, although Jack still received a pension for the remainder of his life and Tina also ended up with a sizeable retirement nest egg of her own, another option they all could have considered was to use life insurance as part of their retirement planning. In fact, a popular technique to potentially maximize pension benefits is the use of life insurance. The process is actually quite simple, as shown by the story of Matt and Colleen.

After serving thirty-five years on the local police force, Matt decided it was time to retire. While reviewing his pension options, he was struggling as to which pension option to choose since he still had two teenagers living at home. He wanted to make sure that his wife and two children could survive financially if he were to die prematurely.

He found the answer in a simple technique: using life insurance.

Matt purchased a life insurance policy, whose proceeds if invested conservatively would provide Colleen and their children a monthly income similar to what his Joint and Survivor pension benefit would have paid.

Instead of choosing the Joint and Survivor pension option, Matt chose the Single Life option, which paid approximately 20 percent more in benefits. He used the difference between the two payments to pay for the insurance policy. So his monthly income remained approximately the same as if he would have chosen the Joint and Survivor option, but with additional benefits to his family.

Instead of being locked into a fixed monthly income, Colleen would get a large lump-sum payment, giving her more flexibility with her finances. For example, if the children were still living at home at home at the time of Matt's death, and the monthly income was not enough to pay all their expenses, she had the ability to tap into the principal to make ends meet or to pay unexpected bills. Had Matt selected the Joint and Survivor pension option, Colleen would have gotten only her regular monthly payments, thereby reducing her financial flexibility.

In addition, if something were to happen to both Matt and Colleen, the Joint and Survivor pension would not have provided anything to the children. The monthly payments would have stopped at the end of both of their lives. With the life insurance, the large lump-sum payment would help ensure that the children were provided for. Life insurance could provide a legacy to all the children. If, for example, Colleen subsequently died after Matt, any remaining amount of the life insurance proceeds would go to their children. With the monthly pension, all benefits would end after Colleen's death, leaving nothing to the children.

While there are some tremendous benefits to using life insurance with a pension benefit, there also are some drawbacks. Matt was able to use this technique because he was in reasonably good health and still young enough to make the premiums affordable. Using insurance with a Single Life pension option would not work with someone in, say, their late sixties or in poor health. This is because they might not qualify for the life insurance or because it could be so expensive that it would cost more than the difference between the Single Life and Joint and Survivor benefit options.

While each person's situation is unique, for most people it is probably worth at least exploring the possibility of using life insurance to maximize pension plan benefits. When faced with the decision of having to choose which pension option to select, make sure you give careful consideration to the people you might leave behind.

Here are some variables to consider when making your decision:

1. The health of both the retiree and the beneficiary, especially if one already has serious health issues
2. The ages of both the retiree and the beneficiary, especially if one is considerably older than the other
3. The income the beneficiary will need
4. The continuing sources of income available to the beneficiary
5. The availability of financial assets to the beneficiary that could generate income at a conservative rate of return
6. Other potential beneficiaries, such as children or ex-spouses, who might expect an inheritance upon the death of the retiree

There are numerous issues to be considered before choosing the optimal pension option. This might well be one of the most important retirement decisions you make when it comes to your finances—and the finances of your beneficiaries. In fact, so important are decisions regarding pensions and pension disbursement that we'll take a deeper look at these issues next, in Chapter 12.

Lessons Learned

- Employees with employer-sponsored pension plans need to decide how to take their monthly payments when they're getting ready to retire. Typically a retiree can choose from a few different monthly retirement benefit options: Single Life, Joint and Survivor, and Period Certain.
- Careful analysis should be done before deciding on a pension option, as your choice will affect your surviving spouse's income depending on what other retirement savings are available.

- Life insurance can be used in conjunction with a pension to augment retirement income and to ensure that your survivor or beneficiary is taken care of financially after you're gone.

CHAPTER 12

Plan for Pension Disbursements

As we saw in the previous chapter, there are numerous decisions to be made when dealing with pensions, even though they have been on the endangered list for some time. However, unlike the Black Rhino, which enjoys endangered species protection, it seems as if the race is on to completely eliminate what used to be the most common retirement income benefit: the defined-benefit pension.

Back in the day, if someone worked for a company for an extended period, it was common to receive a pension, which, along with Social Security benefits, provided a guaranteed stream of income for the employee and his spouse, if married. Then, the couple was able to use whatever savings they had accumulated for discretionary, or lifestyle, expenses such as vacations, presents, and entertainment. However, times have changed. Savings are now a requirement of any successful retirement plan and are no longer used just for discretionary items. In many cases, they have to help pay for basic, fixed expenses.

To illustrate, let's look at two couples who faced important decisions regarding their pensions.

Sally and Bill have been married for thirty years. They have two children, both married, and three grandchildren. They are close to retirement and are looking forward to traveling and spending time with their grandchildren. But Bill recently received a letter that forced them to revisit their plans.

Starting out right after college, Bill worked for Best Widget Corporation for thirty-two years. He then joined Blue Whale Company and has worked for them for the past twelve years. Following college, Sally initially worked full-time, stopped working to raise the children, later returned to part-time work, and for the past fifteen years has worked full-time for Walnut Manufacturing. They both participate in their corporate 401(k) plans, contributing more than the minimum in order to get the maximum match from their employers.

Sally and Bill feel well prepared for retirement. They had developed a retirement plan several years ago with the help of a financial planner and were comfortable with the initial plan, which included a projection of their retirement income starting when Bill turned 66. The plan included a pension from Best Widget Corporation. His current employer had eliminated their pension several years before Bill had joined them, and Sally did not have a pension from her current or former employers.

The letter that Bill received was from the administrator of the Best Widget Corporation pension offering Bill a lump-sum buyout of his pension. He found the number to be quite tempting, but was unsure of how taking the lump sum would affect his overall retirement plan. Calculating the original pension amount as a percentage of the lump-sum offer allowed him to compare the guaranteed pension payment stream to one that could be generated from the lump sum. This gave him a more objective way to evaluate the lump-sum offer.

Bill weighed the advantages of a pension: It provides guaranteed income for a specified time, typically for the life of the pension owner; and the guaranteed payment is typically higher than what can be generated by a lump-sum offer in the current investment environment. On the other hand, there are three major disadvantages of a pension. First, there is no ability to access a lump-sum amount for a major purchase or an emergency. So, if one has a pension, it is critical to have additional savings that can be used in those circumstances. Second, most pensions have no provision for inflation. It is crucial for retired individuals and couples to make sure their retirement plans allow for inflation. Third, selecting the pension over the lump-sum option is a one-time decision and, once that decision is made, it cannot be reversed.

Bill considered that the major advantage of a lump-sum offer is the flexibility to use either the entire amount or some portion of it to pay off debts, make a large purchase, or invest in an annuity, which can provide a pension-like guaranteed income. However, if an annuity is chosen, the payment is typically not as high as the original pension and is always subject to the claims paying ability of the issuing insurance company. Some annuities allow income to be turned on and off, though there may be restrictions that limit when, how often, and over what time period you can turn it on and off. Some annuities also offer inflation hedges, but most do not have any provision for inflation, so you will have a fixed-level benefit that may or may not keep up with the cost of living over time.

Sally and Bill have additional retirement savings that could have complemented Bill's pension, if they had decided to keep it. However, the additional flexibility and freedom that the lump-sum payment provided was attractive enough to them that they chose to exercise the pension buyout. For them, the flexibility of guaranteed income that could be turned on and off, if desired, with access to principal was more attractive than a slightly higher guaranteed income with no ability to stop payments or withdraw principal.

Paula and Marc faced a different question, but one just as critical in terms of their retirement. Paula and Marc have been married for thirty-two years. Paula is 55 years old and has worked full-time at PNG Fluids for the past twelve years after taking time off to raise their children. Marc is 60 years old and just found out that his job has been eliminated. He started working for S&J Metals when they got married and suddenly was out of work. He was upset about the job loss and immediately started a job search, knowing that, at 60 years old, it was going to be challenging to find another job, especially one making the same salary. He had a pension with the company he had just left, as well as a 401(k) plan, so he knew that he could access either account for extra money if he needed it.

Marc knew he was eligible to start the pension, but he didn't know if the monthly benefit would keep growing if he waited to start the payments. He requested a statement from the pension administrator, showing the current pension amount and what the payments would be if he waited until ages 62, 65, or 70 to begin taking his pension. Knowing this information allowed him to reevaluate the retirement plan he had crafted with Paula.

Marc looked at three employment scenarios for the interim until he reached his full retirement age of 66, as defined by the Social Security Administration. .. Working full-time at or below what he was making was the ideal solution. Consulting was something he would do if he needed to, but this was his least favorite option. He started working on all three employment options.

In the meantime, Paula and Marc had another issue to ponder. They did not understand the payment options Marc's pension offered; including Single Life, Joint and Survivor, and Single Life with Period Year Certain (refer back to Chapter 11 for a discussion about pension options). Marc's first instinct was to take the highest-paying option, Single Life; he noticed that the lowest-paying option was 100 percent Joint and Survivor. He and Paula evaluated the three options to determine which was best for them.

Single Life pays Marc for the rest of his life. However, whenever he dies, the monthly pension payments end and are not transferable, making it a dangerous option for Paula. If he starts the pension and dies the next year, Paula doesn't get another dime. This option should be selected with great caution or in concert with a life insurance policy to protect Paula in case of Marc's premature death.

Joint and Survivor comes in different levels, paying Marc a reduced payment for his life in exchange for a slightly lower payment for Paula after his death. Marc can choose 50 percent, 75 percent, or 100 percent. The 100 percent Joint and Survivor is the lowest pension payment option while Marc is alive, as it would continue to pay Paula the same amount if he predeceases her. If Marc outlives Paula, he still gets the same amount for the rest of his life.

The third option is Single Life with Period Year Certain. Like the Single Life and Joint and Survivor benefits, it guarantees a Single Life pension payment for Marc's life as the owner of the pension. However, Marc is able to select a guaranteed minimum number of years that the pension will still be paid to a named beneficiary. The beneficiary does not have to be Paula, though it is most common to name one's spouse. In fact, Paula has to approve any beneficiary other than herself. This is to protect her interest as Marc's spouse. So, if Marc selects a Single Life with 10 Year Period Certain, it will still pay him for the rest of his life. However, if Marc dies in Year 3 and Paula is the named beneficiary, she will receive seven more years of the pension payments; then the payments will stop. The pension will have paid a total of ten years of payments.

Once they understood the various options, Paula and Marc decided it was best to select the 100 percent Joint and Survivor option. They were still deciding on when to start the pension when Marc was offered a full-time job, paying him almost as much as he had been making at his previous employer. He was thrilled and accepted the position, postponing the pension decision until he officially retired at a future date.

For many years, Social Security and pension payments have been the staple income for retired individuals and couples. Times are changing. Social Security is under pressure, and while the government may be forced to modify it at some point in the future, that is likely to be many years from now. The government is typically slow to change social benefit programs despite financial pressure in keeping them afloat.

In contrast, most companies have been proactive and are exploring ways to reduce or eliminate the financial burden that pension plans place on them. As a result, many companies have terminated existing pension plan programs, and few offer pension plans to new employees today. The cost to maintain the guaranteed pension payments keeps increasing as individuals live longer, and the investment returns that pension administrators are able to achieve have been reduced in the low interest rate environment that we are experiencing. Since companies can't just terminate an existing program, they are offering one-time, lump-sum payments in exchange for the company being released from all future pension plan payments to that individual. If the pension plan participant agrees to take a lump-sum payment, the participant is removed from the pension plan, releasing the company from all future financial obligations to that participant.

A final word of caution regarding guaranteed pension payments: a guarantee of payments is only as good as the payer's financial health. If one has questions about the financial health of a pension provider, The stability of a pension should be considered a valid concern only if all three of the following conditions are present:

1. The monthly benefit is far higher than the amount guaranteed by the Pension Benefit Guaranty Corporation (PBGC);
2. The company might go bankrupt in the future; and
3. The pension plan is or will be underfunded when the employer goes bankrupt.

In 2014, the PBGC guaranteed a maximum pension payout of $4,943 per month for a 65-year-old retiree with a Single Life annuity payment or $4,449 for a 50 percent Joint and Survivor annuity. Payment levels are lower, adjusted for age, if the pension is started before age 65.

The laws and regulations governing pensions have changed and continue to evolve. If one is fortunate enough to have a pension plan today, it would be prudent to anticipate the possibility of that pension not being a part of a long-term retirement plan at some point in the future. It is important that alternative plans are developed to avoid any surprises.

Lessons Learned

- Pension plans are under pressure, and many employers are offering current and former employees lump-sum payments in lieu of a lifetime of guaranteed payments. It is important to weigh carefully the options when making a selection.
- Lump-sum payments can be advantageous, including the fact that a lump-sum payment can provide the flexibility to use the money as the pensioner sees fit. Once the lump-sum payment is made, however, the decision is final, and the recipient must budget wisely so the money lasts as long as needed.

- When and how to take pension payments are important considerations. Taking pension payments beginning at ages 62, 65, or 70, and taking the payments as Single Life, Joint and Survivor, or Single Life with Period Year Certain can have a dramatic effect on your finances and must be weighed against your overall financial plan.

CHAPTER 13

Fund Your Future
with Life Insurance

Johnny and Maria are both in their early sixties, still working, and have adult children and a couple of grandchildren. The couple has been careful about saving for retirement, making the most of their defined-contribution plans, protecting against possible exposure to nursing home and long-term care costs, investing in stocks and bonds, and providing a legacy in their memory.

Johnny and Maria have both participated in their respective employers' 401(k) plans for years, Johnny contributing enough every year to at least achieve his company's match. Neither has contributed the maximum to their respective 401(k), so there is room to increase their savings in that regard.

They have no outstanding student loans, they've paid off the mortgage on their house, and they paid off their car loans, too. They are considering opening up and funding a 529 plan for their grandchildren.

The estate plan documentation for Johnny and Maria was well in place. Their wills were current and their healthcare powers of attorney were up to date, and they also had financial powers of attorney arranged. Their beneficiary designations were complete and fully appropriate, listing primary and contingency beneficiaries on their

401(k) plans, their company-sponsored life insurance policies, and their personal life insurance policies, which they've owned for more than thirty years.

Johnny and Maria seemed to have everything in order as far as their finances were concerned. But they still had a question: Could they still attain their retirement goals without necessarily forfeiting their lifestyle? Or, more to the point, could they afford to do all they wished to do during their retirement years?

Johnny and Maria wanted to contribute to their church or charity. They wanted to avoid the drain on resources of an extended stay in a nursing home. They would like to leave something for the children. And, they would like to put idle cash to work.

As they considered where best to invest their money, Johnny and Maria considered whether they should cancel the life insurance policies they've had for the past thirty years. They didn't think the death benefits were needed any longer. Between their company-sponsored life insurance and their 401(k) plans—and because they had just about zero debt—they felt the insurance premiums could be put to better use.

They had, for instance, considered leaving a legacy to their church. One option for them would be to merely change the beneficiary designation on their life insurance policies to the church and make a charitable gift at the time of their death. If there was a cash value to the old policies, Johnny and Maria could elect to donate those dollars upon the surrender of the existing policies. Depending on the type of policy, the cash value in life insurance policies might be available to the insured at the time a policy is surrendered, and in this case, a separate donation is available from the proceeds of the surrender of the policy. This does not apply to term life insurance policies, which, by design, do not build a cash or surrender value.

Another option would be to underwrite a new policy. If they could get approved, Johnny and Maria could make a couple of gifts. Once the church accepted this plan, Johnny and Maria would make the premium payments, now tax deductible, to the church as a donation. The church would become the owner and beneficiary of the policy and would pay the premium with those donation dollars.

In addition to contributing to their church and getting the most out of their life insurance policies, Johnny and Maria wanted to protect themselves against nursing home costs. The cost of a nursing home policy can depend on many variables, the main factors being the benefit amount desired, plus the age and health of the applicant. In addition, Johnny and Maria had to consider issues such as how many months or years of coverage benefit they wanted, how much of a deductible (waiting period) they wanted to assume, and whether they wanted a cost-of-living benefit. Another key concern, of course, was the scenario that neither of them actually went into a nursing home—what would happen to all the premium dollars they'd already paid?

A nursing home insurance policy, though, wasn't their only option. They could, for example, consider making a single payment to an insurance company to buy some similar coverage. This would require an available lump sum of money to redirect to this purpose because the money wasn't needed for income or anticipated other expenses. Sometimes this is known as idle money because it has no known specific purpose attached. Some insurance companies have single premium policies that provide a death benefit, a long-term care or nursing home benefit, and a cash accumulation all in one. There are underwriting guidelines, of course, so health is a major consideration; but if accepted, you could see your savings leveraged by the insurance company to buy different protection options: a death benefit of perhaps twice the amount of the deposit; long-term care benefits that could total as much as six times the amount of the deposit; or earnings of tax-deferred interest.

Another option to securing long-term care allows you to use IRA money to help solve a potential need. For example, let's say that Johnny has an IRA from a rollover he did years ago with a prior company's profit-sharing plan lump-sum distribution. Because Johnny was under age 59½, he chose to have his lump-sum payment sent directly to an IRA custodian. He'd like to do something else with the IRA now, so he applies for a life insurance policy and, after a thorough underwriting, is approved. The current IRA custodian sends his account to the insurance company, which receives the money and uses it to buy an annuity. The annuity then sends an annual payment to the life insurance policy in the form of an IRA distribution, on which taxes are withheld. The net of that distribution buys a life insurance policy on Johnny. So now Johnny has an IRA in the form of an annuity, which is earning interest for him, and a life insurance policy that he owns, which also is earning interest. If Johnny needs long-term care, the insurance policy and the annuity have a dedicated payout for that need, and if it turns out that Johnny never needs long-term care, then, upon his death, his designated beneficiary will receive a tax-free benefit of life insurance. By repositioning an IRA, Johnny could secure long-term care coverage and, in doing so, still not lose control of his money. He could, in fact, spend the money on himself or his family in whatever way he chose.

Insurance policies can be used in other, related ways as well. For instance, Johnny and Maria indicated that they might want to provide something for their grandchildren. Just as they used an insurance policy to protect against long-term care, they could make either a single premium payment to an insurance company or a series of annual premiums into an insurance policy designed to build cash value. The cash value in the policy will earn a market rate of interest on the principal of the deposit, the earnings will be deferred from income taxation, and, with the right combination of events, a loan could be taken on the cash value to provide tax-free money for future use. Policy owners have the right to take loans against policy values, which are otherwise known as cash or surrender value. The interest rates on policy loans are often better than the rates that are available on consumer loans or lines of credit. The loan itself is received as a tax-free distribution to the owner or the insured.

Paying back loans can be done with a structured format or not. If a loan is not repaid, the death benefit is reduced by the amount of loan and accrued interest at the time of the claim. This allows access to saved money for emergencies or can serve as income supplement for the owner.

Life insurance is not limited to income replacement or death benefits. It can be used to create an estate, fund a charity, shelter unearned income from excess taxes, or even hedge against nursing-home expenses. Although as you age you might wonder whether you still need the death benefit of life insurance, you could use this financial tool in any number of other ways to help you achieve your financial goals.

Of course, there are other useful insurance-related tools as well, and among them is healthcare insurance. We'll look at that next, in Chapter 14.

Lessons Learned

- As you age, it becomes important to take stock of your finances, investments, and insurance policies, making sure that they are continuing to meet your needs and your goals.
- Don't cancel a life insurance policy as you age simply because you believe you won't need the death benefit. Instead, investigate other ways that you can turn your life insurance policy into a financial tool that works for you.
- Life insurance policies can be structured in ways that go well beyond providing income replacement or a lump-sum death benefit. They can be used to orchestrate donations, secure long-term care, and provide loans at highly competitive interest rates.

CHAPTER 14

Consider Your Health When Planning for the Future

Most of us tend to take our health for granted. We also tend to believe that we likely will mirror our family history. In many instances, that turns out to be the case. However, none of us can predict how our lives will develop or how healthy we will be during our time on Earth.

Let's look at Jessie and Clark. At 57 years old, Clark had a good job and was happily married to Jessie. They were both happy, healthy, and active. They expected to work until Clark turned 66, his full retirement age according to the Social Security Administration.

When he turned 57, Clark visited his primary care physician for his annual physical. Everything was normal, except for his blood test, which showed elevated levels of prostate-specific antigen. The physician recommended a prostate exam as a precautionary measure. The urologist found everything to be normal, except for a small amount of soft tissue. He recommended a biopsy, again as a precautionary step. Two weeks later, the urologist called to inform Clark that he had prostate cancer.

Clark was shocked. He knew that his side of the family had a history of cancer—his father died of colon cancer at age 66, and his mother was a thirty-year survivor of breast cancer before passing away at age 85. But he had been so careful, eating healthy foods, exercising, and getting an annual physical so he could avoid what happened to his parents. It was good news that they had discovered it early as he was quite aware of what could happen if it wasn't caught early enough.

Clark certainly did not expect to be concerned about his health at age 57. He was fortunate in that prostate cancer has a very high cure rate, if caught early. Since they did catch it early, he evaluated his options, chose surgery, and was out of work for two weeks. He felt fortunate as this was hardly an interruption compared to what most people affected by cancer have to deal with, between the various tests, procedures, surgeries, treatments, and office visits.

Because of his family history, Clark was aware of the possibility of getting cancer, or any other major illness, but he and Jessie had never given much thought about the financial impact of a major illness on their finances. Jessie's parents had been fortunate, not having had any major illness before they passed away, her mother at age 86, and her father at age 84. They had lived a very comfortable life and also left a small inheritance.

Clark's parents never discussed their financial matters with him, though they seemed to handle their expenses with little difficulty. They had lived a very comfortable life, and when they passed away, there was a small inheritance. At the time, Clark didn't think much about it. He never knew how much of his parents' retirement savings had been spent on medical expenses associated with the cancer surgeries and treatments. He thought that Medicare had covered all of those expenses, but he was wrong.

When Clark found out he had cancer, he was devastated, as most people are when they first find out such tragic news. He and Jessie met with the doctors and discussed the various treatments and chose surgery. It was successful, and no follow-up treatment was required. He did not need chemotherapy or radiation at all. He recovered physically, but the experience forever affected his view of the future. Reflecting on his parents, his research about the various types of cancer made him realize that his parents had undoubtedly spent much more money on their healthcare needs than he had originally thought and must have been well prepared for retirement to have so successfully navigated that period in their life.

This is not always the case when one learns of having a serious illness. Susan was single, working full-time for large manufacturing company and planning to retire at age 66, her full retirement age according to Social Security. She had done a good job saving for retirement, and when she met with a financial planner, the retirement planning confirmed it. When she turned 65, she signed up for Medicare and, since she was healthy, she signed up for Medicare Advantage, a healthcare plan that takes care of expenses that Medicare does not pay and includes a prescription drug plan. So, she was well prepared for retirement when she retired at 66.

One year later, she learned that she had breast cancer. Aside from the stress associated with all of the tests, procedures, surgeries, and office visits, Susan learned that she was restricted to the network offered by the Medicare Advantage plan provider she chose. She found that the plan limited which hospital she could go to and which doctors she could see. More importantly, when she visited her sister in Florida and needed to see a doctor while there, she found out that it was quite expensive to visit an "out of network" doctor.

After this experience, Susan contacted her insurance agent and asked to review her options. She learned that she could choose a supplemental plan that would have higher costs associated with it than the Advantage plan but would have no out-of-pocket cost to see a doctor, including the doctor practicing in Florida. This plan was attractive to her, but she learned that there was a high probability of being denied based on her preexisting condition. Depending on the insurance carrier, she would have to wait until she satisfied the look-back period, which could be up to five years. In the meantime, she would have to keep her Advantage plan and pay for any out-of-network procedures, surgeries, and office visits.

Susan is doing great now. She is happy and healthy, and has a robust head of hair once again. She is enjoying her retirement even more since the cancer scare made her look at life through a different lens than she did before.

It's hard to anticipate everything that can happen in life, but it's worth considering strategies if certain things do happen. Although Susan had not specifically planned for the expenses associated with the cancer treatments that were not covered by Medicare Advantage, she had built in some financial contingencies that provided enough funds to allow her to weather the financial storm. Anticipating the possibility of emergencies or major illnesses can provide the financial freedom to choose the best option for your health when an event actually occurs. Knowing that you have this flexibility in your retirement plan can provide you with extra peace of mind, which comes in handy when you do face an unexpected event of this type.

Both Clark and Susan were surprised when they first learned of their cancer. Generally, we tend to downplay the possibility of contracting a major illness. It happens to others—not to us. No one builds a plan with the expectation that they will have a major illness at a certain age. When it happens, it surprises us. Although we cannot predict if or when a major illness may strike us, we can anticipate a major financial surprise and plan for that possibility. Best case, it never comes to fruition; worst case, it is a contingency covered by the plan.

Healthcare planning, long-term care insurance, life insurance—all of that should be part of a sound, comprehensive financial plan. No one knows what could happen in life—and anything could occur at any time. It's best to plan for health-related eventualities, even if doing so might be uncomfortable. But it's important to plan for the future. Along with saving, investing, and buying insurance, that includes creating an estate plan to protect your legacy. We'll look at that next, in Chapter 15.

Lessons Learned

- Healthcare planning should be part of everyone's comprehensive financial planning, not just those whose family histories include illness or disease.
- Healthcare planning should include rainy day funds, income-protection instruments, long-term care insurance, nursing home insurance, and so on.
- Everyone should take the time to understand the nuances of various Medicare plans as well as the differences between Medicare and Medicaid.

CHAPTER 15

Control Your Legacy

It would be wonderful to have a crystal ball. As we've seen, Clark and Susan would have loved to have had one with which to foretell their futures so they could better navigate their health scares.

With a crystal ball we could learn of market corrections before they occurred, and we could reallocate our portfolios accordingly. We would know the day, time, and cause of our demise. About a week prior to our last day on Earth, we could retitle our assets and leave envelopes for our spouses and children with instructions as to what they've received, how they've received it, and what they should do going forward. In addition, we could buy life insurance at the best possible time to ensure that we pay the least amount in premiums in return for the greatest potential benefit. Life would be grand, and we could be certain that everyone would be provided for after we're gone. We would be in complete control of our legacies.

Unfortunately, none of us has a crystal ball that can really help with such matters. In fact, as is often said, there are only two certainties in life: death and taxes. Although we may frequently tell our children otherwise, we know that we really are mortal and at some point our time here will be up. Proper diet and exercise might reduce many of the risks that we might otherwise face, but they certainly won't help us avoid getting hit by a distracted driver or being struck by a falling tree.

In fact, death before our calculated life expectancy occurs so frequently that we should all consider the possibility of not living to be 76 or 81 years. And by considering such a possibility, perhaps we can take better control of our legacies—that, indeed, would almost be like having the proverbial crystal ball.

Young professionals and preretirees often believe that estate planning is something for old people to do and that they have plenty of time before they will have to consider doing it themselves. Oftentimes, younger folks either don't want to bother with estate planning because they don't perceive a real benefit or they simply put off thinking about the eventuality of their own demise. For others, estate planning is something for "rich folks," and in their minds, they simply don't qualify.

Unfortunately, too many people plan to get their affairs in order tomorrow without realizing that tomorrow never comes. When no estate plan is in place, the probate process is lengthy, cumbersome, and dissatisfying. Many such situations could easily be avoided with just a little bit of effort and planning.

Estate planning for the preretiree can be as complicated or as simple as the individual desires. We can throw around terms like *family limited partnerships, intentionally defective grantor trusts with self-canceling installment notes, marital trusts, irrevocable life insurance trusts,* and *qualified personal residence trusts,* but such concepts are often well beyond the comprehension—or interest—of most individuals. Such financial planning instruments might seem helpful and important, but they also can paralyze people into doing nothing.

In estate planning, this can be disastrous.

Simply put, the primary objective of an estate plan should be to put the largest amount of an individual's assets into the hands of his or her loved ones as fast as possible with the least amount of disruption to their lives. Secondary considerations might include mitigating tax consequences and instituting spendthrift provisions for those beneficiaries who might not be in a position to protect themselves from making impulsive or ill-advised financial decisions.

When we consider our passing, we envision our loved ones looking back upon our lives with great joy. We want them to be able to grieve without enduring any financial hardships. We don't want the image of our lives to be clouded by the memory of difficulties transferring assets to beneficiaries, delays from the probate process, or our spouse's diminished standard of living owing to our poor choices or procrastination. We certainly don't want to be the subject of gossip at the local coffee shop: "He was a great guy, but did you hear about what happened after he died?" With a little effort, everyone can avoid this.

Dave and Maureen provide a good example of the importance of estate planning. They were the perfect couple. They started courting in high school and continued dating while Dave served in the U.S. Marine Corps. Shortly after Dave was honorably discharged, they were married. After thirty-one happy years of marriage, they had raised three wonderful children and were anticipating the birth of their second grandchild. They were not materially wealthy, but their love for one another was inspiring. Dave worked in transportation, and Maureen worked at home until their kids were old enough to be at home by themselves. In their leisure time, they would tend to their own family garden and frequent state parks for camping, hiking, and taking nature walks. Life in their household was pretty simple, and spending quality time together was the focus for everyone in the family.

Some time ago, Dave and Maureen had purchased a modest house in the suburbs. They considered it their dream home, and each of the children spent much of their childhood in this home. The family enjoyed visiting with the neighbors and attending block parties, and they never contemplated living anywhere else. Dave used his Veteran benefits to assist in financing the house and, consequently, financed the home in his name alone, although the house was titled jointly. Maureen was creditworthy for a mortgage, but the couple decided it was advantageous to avoid the down payment by utilizing Dave's VA benefits.

A few years ago, Dave's position was terminated with his employer. To make matters worse, the value of the home had dropped to nearly $50,000 less than what they owed on it. Dave subsequently found another job. He then applied for a loan modification with his lender and ultimately was approved. The couple was blessed: The bank would adjust the mortgage to the current market value of the home and even reduce the monthly payment. Dave received the paperwork in the mail and simply had to sign the modification, have it notarized, and return it to the lender. Things were really looking up for them.

Within a few weeks of receiving the modification paperwork in the mail, Dave was involved in a tragic accident at work. His injuries were so severe that they ultimately cost him his life. Dave had created a living will, and he had also executed a health care power of attorney in which he designated Maureen as his healthcare surrogate. Maureen had to make the unenviable decision of removing Dave from life support per his wishes as expressed in his living will. Had she not been able to do so, Dave would not have been allowed to pass with the dignity he desired, and the cost of care could have been financially catastrophic for Maureen and their family.

Dave had designated Maureen as the beneficiary of his employer-sponsored group term life insurance and his qualified retirement plans, a 401(k) and an IRA. These assets transferred to Maureen rather quickly and without restriction. The value of the insurance was not enough to make Maureen wealthy, but it was enough to give her a bit of a nest egg. A claim was also filed through Ohio Bureau of Workers' Compensation in an effort to further provide for Maureen. The likelihood of the claim being successful was uncertain, as was the time horizon and manner in which it would be paid out. As a result, Maureen had reason to be concerned about cash flow in the short term, when all she really wanted to worry about was grieving the loss of her husband and best friend.

While going through paperwork at their desk, Maureen noticed that the loan modification paperwork for their home had never been signed or sent to the lender. She couldn't sign the paperwork, as doing so would be fraudulent, so she called the bank to ask what her options were. The bank wouldn't discuss the issue with her because she was not on the mortgage. She'd have to open an estate through the local Probate Court and be appointed as administrator of Dave's estate. After doing so, Maureen learned that the approval of the loan modification expired upon Dave's death. As the surviving spouse, she could refinance the home in her name, but she would need to make a down payment of $50,000. This represented the difference between the amount owed and the fair market value of the home. Not knowing the likelihood of the workers' compensation claim and having limited liquid funds available to her, Maureen couldn't justify spending so much of her nest egg to keep a house that wasn't retaining its value. Accordingly, Maureen had to abandon the home.

Maureen might not have remained in the home even if she had been able to obtain the modification. As she often put it, "Dave is in every corner of this house, and it is too painful." Regardless, she didn't really have a choice. To preserve her nest egg while waiting for the workers' compensation claim to be adjudicated, she moved into a three-bedroom apartment that she shared with her daughter and granddaughter. It was a nice apartment, but she didn't have the amount of living space, storage, or neighbors that she had become accustomed to. This resulted in a significant disruption to her life, on top of losing Dave, and it caused her much angst when all she really wanted to do was grieve the loss of her husband.

Maureen eventually received an order from workers' compensation in the amount of more than $1 million, payable monthly over her life. (A wrongful death action is still pending.) After the passage of a year since Dave's death, she considers the monthly payment from workers' compensation as part of Dave's legacy, as is the shadow box filled with his Marine Corps dress uniform. She misses Dave terribly, as do their children; but even after death, he is still taking care of her.

From an estate planning perspective, Dave did many things right. He provided beneficiary designations on his life insurance and qualified retirement accounts. The house was titled jointly. He had a will, and although none of the assets passed through it, he nominated Maureen as administrator of his estate, making it that much easier for her to be appointed quickly. And by having a Living will and health care power of attorney, he was able to allow Maureen to make on his behalf the decisions he wanted to be made. The only shortcoming was that he didn't immediately sign the loan modification and, therefore, provide for Maureen to afford to continue to live in the house, if she chose to do so. This created an unnecessary disruption to her life.

Estate planning isn't merely about document creation for the elderly. Estate planning has more to do with ensuring a seamless transition of assets than it does with drafting special documents and should be part of an overall financial plan. In addition to protecting legacies, everyone should consider not only which assets will pass to whom and how they will pass, but also how the assets will be retained by the beneficiary. Oftentimes, retention of the asset is the key, and it is the element most overlooked. Estate planning can help mitigate these issues.

No one has a crystal ball. We can't see what the future brings. Having an estate plan in place can help us—and those we love—deal with all the various issues that surround our assets and our legacies. Planning for the future is important at all stages of life—crystal ball or not. Whether it's dealing with the discomfort of our eventual demise or dealing with more immediate crises, such as job loss, planning is crucial if you want to retire well. We'll examine that a bit more, in Chapter 16.

Lessons Learned

- Estate planning is often overlooked for any number of reasons, none of them sound. Because it's so easy to put off today what could be done tomorrow, too many people find that tomorrow never comes or that it comes too late, leaving their legacies unprotected.
- Estate planning should include such things as wills and living wills, health care power of attorney, asset distribution, and beneficiary designations on life insurance and qualified retirement accounts.
- It's important to name someone as administrator of the estate, which helps the probate process go more smoothly and more quickly—and less painfully—for everyone.

CHAPTER 16

Insure Yourself Against the Unexpected

Job loss, a health crisis, even sudden death: any of us can be taken by surprise by an unexpected downturn of one kind or another. These unforeseen events can be painful, no matter what the cause or when they happen, and they can force us to change our lives in ways we never anticipated.

For example, the Great Recession of 2008–09 accelerated early retirement planning for numbers of Americans, many not of their own volition. Massive corporate layoffs thrust millions of Americans into transition status.

Many of us associate 65 with the age of retirement (retirement at a younger age is usually referred to as early retirement or preretirement). When faced with the notion of an unexpected or unwanted job loss over fifty, the first reaction of many individuals is to update their resume, dust off their contact list, join as many networking groups as possible, search online job boards, and look for the next great opportunity. Generally, individuals try to preserve the status quo, going to the same kind of job, doing the same kinds of things, making the same kind of money. For some, this plan works. For many in the over-fifty crowd during the Great Recession, such was not the case.

Barbara lost her job in 2008. She was 62 years old and single. Losing her job was traumatic. She felt social and economic pressure to replace her job, and her income as soon as possible. She desperately sought full-time employment while utilizing unemployment benefits and all of the possible benefit extensions available at the time. Without a specific accounting of her financial status, she assumed that she needed to work until the normal retirement age of 65. She figured that once she made it to 65, she could start Social Security, sign up for Medicare, and enjoy her retirement years.

However, that new job—the one just like she used to have, the one that would bridge the gap to age 65—was not materializing. In the interim, she took part-time jobs, balancing her earnings with the unemployment benefits she was receiving.

At the time she had lost her job, she had been working with an advisor who was providing investment advice but not assisting her with overall financial planning or helping with her job search. She was concerned about her loss of income, and watching her investments go down in value during the Great Recession added to her anxiety. The advisor was not making any changes to the portfolio he was managing, even though she kept expressing her concerns about the declining value. Along with that concern were those to find employment and to contribute; she felt too young to retire.

Though Barbara had not done any official retirement planning with her investment advisor, she had always lived below her means, resulting in her having a fair amount of retirement savings. She had no idea of how well prepared she actually was—or was not—for retirement, and the advisor she was working with was doing nothing to help relieve her stress. She didn't know what to do about her investments, so she just kept working on what she could control: the job search and how to keep qualifying for unemployment benefits until she found a new position.

Finally Barbara made a few calculations, and it soon became clear that she had actually done a pretty good job of building a nest egg and that, at least on the surface, her situation didn't look as bleak as she thought. Although she didn't have an abundant amount of assets, it appeared that what she did have in her portfolio would be sufficient to support her lifestyle.

While she appreciated hearing that message, she still didn't trust the analysis that showed her that she was financially able to retire, so she continued to search for a new job to replace her income. In the meantime, she worked part-time to generate income and volunteered so she could also otherwise contribute to society. Unfortunately, she also continued to experience a high degree of anxiety.

Finally, a year later, Barbara started to believe that she might be better prepared for retirement than she originally had thought. She continued to update the analysis and she continued to ask questions, building confidence along the way. At the same time, the unemployment benefits extensions were coming to an end. She was still feeling very anxious.

Unfortunately, shortly after her unemployment benefits ended, she learned that she had cancer. Her job-search stress was soon replaced with an even higher level of stress due to her cancer diagnosis. Now, the focus became her health and survival, to knowing what was happening to her body and how far the cancer might have spread.

Having developed confidence in a new financial plan, she entertained the possibility that once she got through the surgery and was fully recovered, she could plan a great trip that had long been on her bucket list. Thinking about the trip was inspirational and gave her something to look forward to after her recovery.

She survived her cancer treatments and began embracing a new, more balanced view of life. She did plan that trip, and she felt confident living the comfortable life she had been preparing for financially. She worked with her financial planner to include room in her retirement plan for vacations, home improvements, and even a new car. She also set up realistic budgets so she could spend freely within her allowances without stressing out or feeling nervous about spending her money.

More detailed financial planning could have relieved some of the stress she experienced while looking for a job, anxiety that possibly contributed to some of the health issues that developed. Having a better sense of her own financial freedom might have unburdened Barbara of some of the worry that so affected her.

Financial freedom is about more than having a big bank account. It's about knowing how well prepared you are for the future so that you can retire well. No one knows exactly what the future holds, but the better prepared you are, the more comfortable you can be that your retirement years will be spent just as you hope they will be.

Preparation includes investment planning, healthcare planning, estate planning, and overall financial planning, all geared to helping you enjoy a comfortable retirement. Whether you expect to work to your Social Security–authorized retirement age or into your seventies, you intend to volunteer your time after you quit working, or you find your career status altered unexpectedly by a layoff or job loss, planning can provide you with the kind of financial freedom that makes such transitions more palatable. In fact, we'll look more closely at this in Chapter 17.

Lessons Learned

- Sudden unemployment, for whatever reason, can cause a great deal of stress, regardless of whether you've retired or lost your job unwillingly. Having a financial plan in place ahead of time can help ease the stress of transitioning to this new period in your life.

- Although finding a job might be your first, knee-jerk response to losing your position, if you're close to retirement, you might consider whether early retirement is financially feasible for you. Severance packages, pensions, Social Security benefits, and Medicare benefits might well add up to enough resources to support the lifestyle you want.

- Unexpected changes in life—whether job loss or a catastrophic health issue—drive home the need for a rainy day fund. Be sure to include allowance in your financial planning for income that will help you weather the storm.

CHAPTER 17

Manage Income Disruptions

As we saw in the previous chapter, Barbara was surprised—and somewhat unprepared—when she lost her job. That was, indeed, a bad day for her. We all have bad days. For some of us, it involves sleeping past the alarm and being late to work. For others, just finding out that they're out of coffee in the morning can really set the stage for a day of misery.

But there are bad days—and then there are really bad days. A really bad day involves getting tragic news or experiencing a loss that forever shapes the direction in which your life is headed. The severity of the pain we feel is largely dependent upon our reaction to the loss, but this is often difficult to immediately understand.

Keith and Cheryl had a really bad day in 2009. Both were age 55, and they had been happily married for more than thirty years. Keith was a marketing executive with a global corporation who was repeatedly recognized as a star in his field. Cheryl had a background in accounting, but had elected to stay at home and run their household. This was no small task.

Once their children were grown and had careers of their own, Keith and Cheryl moved around quite a bit as Keith's employer would send him from one facility to the next to "work his magic" and right the proverbial ship. The work was at times exhausting, and both were looking forward to the day when they could retire and travel to places they actually wanted to go and visit with their families. Cheryl wanted to spend weeks at a time visiting their children and, with any luck, grandchildren.

For them, age 62 seemed to be the perfect age to retire. Keith was earning a six-figure income, and they were really beginning to save enough money to make retirement at age 62 a reality. In addition, they planned to sell their home and move into a condo. The proceeds of the sale would allow them to buy the condo outright and leave them with additional funds to contribute to their nest egg. Keith and Cheryl were living the American Dream—until they had a really bad day.

The day had started out like many others for Keith. He read the morning paper and spent time checking up on his beloved football team, the New York Giants. After chatting with Cheryl, he ventured off to his office where the day veered in a different direction. A team of human resource professionals from the home office was conducting one-on-one interviews with many of the staff. Keith had heard rumors of changes taking place within the company, but he had never been very concerned about the outcome. In Keith's mind, change was always taking place, and his performance reviews were such that he really didn't feel like he had reason to worry. After all, he had been through countless "initiatives" that were recommended by various consulting firms, and, after weathering each storm of change, things would return to the way they had been before. More than anything else, Keith was worried about his friends and colleagues, the ones who, unlike Keith, didn't have personnel files full of glowing reviews and countless examples quotas exceeded based on revenue generated.

Until it was time for his own interview with HR.

During Keith's interview, HR discussed the global recession and represented the significant negative impact it was having on his employer. He was told that many positions were being eliminated in order for the company to be able to adapt and survive in the ever-changing global marketplace. One such position, he learned, was his own. After a recent acquisition, his employer was left with much overlap in various areas, and it was necessary to consolidate the responsibilities of multiple executives in order to streamline efficiency and thrive in the years to come. Although they told Keith he had been seriously considered for this new role, his employer had decided to go in a different direction. Keith would be given six months of severance pay, and he was offered three months of outplacement services during which he could work on his resume and attend job search workshops. Keith was asked to turn in all property belonging to his employer, collect his personal belongings, and leave the facility. As he was escorted from the premises, to say that he was in shock would be an understatement.

No one was more surprised than Cheryl to see Keith come home early that day. When he told her the news, she cried. She, too, felt shock and, to an extent, grief. But their responses to the crisis were dramatically different. Keith was worried about his next venture. He knew that he would land on his feet; he just didn't know when and where. He would be collecting a paycheck for the next six months, but knew he had to start looking for a job right away. He immediately began scouring his contacts on LinkedIn and in his Rolodex to see if anyone in his network was in need of the marketing expertise he could provide.

Cheryl, on the other hand, was worried about their dreams, asking herself questions like "How will we pay the mortgage?" and "Can we even afford groceries?" As the days passed, she started wondering if they'd ever be able to retire and whether they'd be able to see their kids over the holidays, as they had planned to do.

Keith was focused on landing a new job, but Cheryl was focused on survival. Both were afraid, but for different reasons. Luckily, they were able to communicate their feelings with one another and were intent on developing a strategy together.

The days of Keith's transition turned to months, and he soon realized that many of the employers for which he would like to work had established hiring freezes. Worse yet, many of the contacts who might be able to assist him were also in the job market themselves. To further his job search, Keith attended the outplacement sessions regularly and with enthusiasm, and he joined several networking groups. He met each new day with optimism, which seemed to provide comfort for Cheryl.

Keith's severance was paid in the form of a lump sum. In addition, the unemployment compensation that Keith collected, while merely a percentage of Keith's former salary, allowed the couple to save some of his severance pay for a later date. Their lifestyle changed, though not as significantly as Cheryl had feared. There were always groceries in the pantry, and the couple never skipped a meal. They did, however, stop eating out. They even made a game out of being frugal and saving money. This enabled them to feel more connected than ever, and they really felt like were working together toward a common goal. Working together, something they had never considered doing outside of managing the household, seemed to be quite fulfilling.

Keith attended an outplacement session on franchising and, as a result, his job search took a dramatic turn. Rather than search for a job, he thought, why not create one? He had always been entrepreneurial and began to wonder if working for himself might be the best option available to him. After it seemed that he was being confronted with roadblocks at every turn in his job search, his focus began to shift more toward starting his own business. There was really only one person he had to convince: Cheryl.

Keith was a risk taker by nature. Cheryl, on the other hand, was not. Cheryl had become accustomed to security. She knew what the fixed expenses in the household were each month, and she relied upon Keith's paycheck every month to meet those expenses. Keith's annual bonus had been usually devoted to savings, and it had provided "fun money" for them to travel. This routine had been reassuring for her. The thought of deviating from this routine caused Cheryl a great deal of anxiety—and rightly so. After all, it would be very difficult to create a household budget if she had no idea as to how much money would be coming in each month. In order to reassure Cheryl, Keith needed an objective ally.

Keith attended a financial planning session called "Managing Your Finances in Career Transition" at the outplacement firm. The multifaceted approach discussed in the session appealed to Keith, who decided it was time to discuss options with Cheryl and a financial planner.

During that meeting, Keith recounted the recent turn of events that had shifted his focus from being a full-time employee to the prospect of starting his own business. Keith had a lot of questions, and Cheryl had a lot of concerns. Keith asked questions like "Can we afford to start our own business and not derail our retirement objectives? If we start our own business, should I be a marketing consultant or should we buy a franchise? Should we create an entity? What type of lawyer and accountant would we need?"

Cheryl interrupted his questions with one of her own: "How will we eat, and where will we live?"

When it came to their finances, Keith and Cheryl had much to be proud of. Their personal savings account contained several hundred thousand dollars. Keith had regularly contributed to the 401(k) offered through his previous employer and had accumulated a balance of more than $500,000. In addition, Keith had a vested defined-benefit plan, or pension, from his employer that, upon reaching the age of 65, would provide him with several thousand dollars each month for the rest of his life. Should he predecease Cheryl, it would pay her either 50 or 75 percent of his benefit, whichever he selected, for the rest of her lifetime. Moreover, while their home had an existing mortgage, they did own significant equity. Taking all of their assets into account, Keith and Cheryl had accumulated more than $1 million.

A million dollars might sound like a lot, but whether it actually is depends on how long you need it to last and how much you plan on spending each year in retirement. If someone desires an income of $200,000 each year, then $1 million will likely not last very long. In Keith and Cheryl's case, they desired a modest, though not insignificant, amount to live off each year from their retirement nest egg. After taking into consideration their projected Social Security benefits and Keith's pension, they focused on determining how much they would need to withdraw each year in order to meet their retirement income goals, based on various life expectancies. They chose 100 percent Joint and Survivor, which means the pension would be paid to them as long either one of them are alive, so even if Keith dies first, Cheryl is provide for.

Keith and Cheryl considered several scenarios with various rates of return and settled upon an income they were comfortable with. This aspect of the calculation was critical because it helped establish risk parameters for their portfolio and provided a basis against which to check progress. It also helped them determine how much they could set aside for the new business and how much they could personally live off of without jeopardizing their retirement lifestyle.

Having established how much money could be allocated to the business, Keith and Cheryl then had to determine what the business would look like. Keith's niche was marketing, but he was well versed in various aspects of sales and operations as well. He could create "Keith's Marketing LLC" and act as a consultant or project manager for several companies. Doing so would require little overhead, and the funds devoted to the business could be stretched further, but he feared that the business wouldn't be "sellable" when it was time to retire or in the event of Keith's death.

As such, Keith feared that instead of creating an asset, he would merely be buying himself a job. Cheryl, to her credit, was less than thrilled with the idea that Keith might have projects that required him to be away from home for extended periods of time. If they were going to do this, she wanted it to be as successful as possible, which might mean looking for clients outside the region. After more than thirty years of marriage, they still thoroughly enjoyed spending time together, and this period of transition had brought them even closer together. They were working toward a common goal and extensive work-related travel would create a scenario that neither would be comfortable with. Besides, they found that they really enjoyed working together.

After much discussion and research, Keith and Cheryl decided to pursue a franchise that would provide both tangible goods and valuable services to their clients. In doing so, they'd create multiple streams of revenue for the entity. They settled on a particular franchise and calculated the cost of the purchase, operating costs, as well as other miscellaneous expenses, such as health care for both of them. To provide further assurance, they set aside funds in a separate brokerage account that would pay their personal expenses for a specified period of time. They also determined how to contribute to the business in order to provide enough seed money for several years.

Once they had that figured out, they turned to considering how the business would be run. They decided that Keith would handle marketing and sales and Cheryl would handle accounts payable and accounts receivable. In addition, they would need one employee at the outset to handle customer service.

There was just one small detail left to tackle: how to finance ongoing operating costs until the business could function on its own.

Keith and Cheryl soon learned that some of their assets were not going to be able to help them finance the business. For instance, although they had substantial equity in their home, they would not be able to obtain a home equity line of credit from a bank because they did not have a verifiable stream of income. Banks were, however, willing to lend them funds that were secured by either a savings or a brokerage account, but this seemed untenable to Keith and Cheryl. For them, it felt like they would be paying interest on their own money, which just didn't seem fair.

As an alternative, Keith could withdraw funds from his 401(k) without penalty because he was over the age of 55. Many people don't realize that you can take money from a 401(k) as early as age 55 and still avoid the 10 percent early withdrawal penalty, unlike with an IRA where you have to be a minimum of age 59½. First, although they would avoid the 10 percent penalty on the withdrawal, the funds would still represent taxable income, and they didn't want to incur taxes on a calculated risk they were taking. Second, Keith's former employer's plan did not allow for partial distributions for those who were separated from employment. Thus, he could either withdraw the entire amount or none of it, and they weren't willing to pay tax on the entire amount. Finally, he could roll it into an IRA, which he ultimately chose to do, even though he was subject to a 10 percent penalty on withdrawals because he was under the age of 59½. As such, they decided that it was in their best interest to finance the business via a loan from their personal savings. If and when the business became profitable, it would then systematically pay them back. This bucket of assets was created for them with the understanding that when the bucket was empty, either the business was functioning on its own or Keith would be polishing his resume and seeking employment elsewhere. To do otherwise would jeopardize their retirement lifestyle more than they were comfortable with.

After acquiring the franchise, creating a corporate entity for it, and providing a bucket from which to operate the business, the real fun could begin. The day-to-day operation of the business has been fulfilling for Keith and Cheryl, but also quite stressful. They've had to endure expenses that could not necessarily be foreseen. Some expenses were blessings, such as the cost of utilizing temping agencies for staffing needs when demand exceeded capacity. Other expenses, though, such as a dramatic increase in the cost of health insurance, served as temporary setbacks for them at the most inopportune times. Keith had been eligible for continued health insurance coverage from his former employer under the COBRA law at the time the business was acquired. The cost of the insurance, however, soon became unmanageable and they had to explore other options. Both were in good health, so they opted to select a health insurance plan that had a higher deductible but required a lower monthly payment. This cost savings allowed Keith and Cheryl to stretch the funds in the business bucket.

Another expense that was difficult to prepare for was the cost of goods that would be sold to their clients. After all, sending an invoice to a client does not necessarily insure prompt payment, and some clients pay more promptly than others. In short, each client's invoice cycle was different, which had to be accounted for—and managed.

This occasionally created cash flow concerns that, while manageable, were stressful. Perhaps the greatest hardship to the business occurred when a trusted employee decided to accept a new position that was closer to his home. His new employer expected him to start immediately, and he quit without notice. The business had several projects that had yet to be completed at the time, and so, while interviewing prospective employees, Keith and Cheryl had to hire contractors at a rate that was more than double what they were accustomed to paying an employee. For many new businesses, this could have been the death knell, but Keith and Cheryl stuck to the plan of utilizing only the funds allocated to the business. It would have been easy to tap into their personal savings, but once they strayed from the business bucket, it would be that much easier to do it again and again. Had they done so, they may not have been able to emerge unscathed when it was time for retirement.

Throughout the endeavor, two things have remained constant: Keith and Cheryl thoroughly enjoy working together, and they haven't extended their personal investment beyond the bucket of funds originally devoted to the business. In fact, a personal triumph occurred when the business was able to obtain its own line of credit. Today, the business is profitable, and Keith and Cheryl are being repaid on the loan that they made. The real surprise from this venture, considering the terror that she expressed at first, is how calm Cheryl has been during stressful times for the business. She has been the reassuring voice of reason throughout and has provided Keith with the same sense of security that Cheryl desperately needed at the outset.

Keith and Cheryl have done well for themselves. No doubt they also would have been successful had Keith decided to become a freelance marketing consultant while working on multiple projects for various clients. But they chose to go in a different direction in order to create a joint asset that can survive either of them. It isn't necessarily the right choice for every situation, but it was right for them. They're now in a position that they are receiving inquiries from individuals about the possibility of buying the franchise. They're seriously considering it, particularly because they are approaching age 62 and want to retire as planned. They're also considering it because they became grandparents a year ago. Both are ready to call in sick because there is some place else they'd rather be. That's a pretty good sign that it is time to convert the asset they created together.

Whenever they do decide to sell, the proceeds from their business will enhance their lifestyle, in large part because they never put their retirement in jeopardy. In short, their reaction to that very bad day years ago was careful and methodical, and it has led to greater fulfillment in their lives.

Bad days can strike at any time, and we can never be certain of the future. If you seek out the knowledge of what your financial profile looks like going forward, it can help you adjust your current lifestyle in order to be better prepared for tomorrow. This is true whether dealing with an unexpected change in your employment status, a health issue, or even divorce. We'll look at divorce next, in Chapter 18.

Lessons Learned

- Losing a job and having to start over can be an unnerving prospect at any age, and perhaps especially so for individuals who are nearing retirement. Those who have sound financial plans in place are better positioned to weather the storm.
- In addition to a rainy day fund, other resources to ride out unexpected disruptions in income are severance packages, pension distributions, 401(k) withdrawals, home equity lines of credit, or other financial instruments—but be sure to carefully consider the pros and cons of each.
- Starting a new business during the twilight of your career can be fulfilling and enriching—and stressful. Consider issues such as what your typical workday will look like, how you will fund the business, how you will handle downturns, and how much income you expect.

CHAPTER 18

Deal Carefully with Divorce (and Remarriage)

Just as most of us never really expect to get laid off or suffer a catastrophic illness, no one goes into marriage expecting it to fail. But we all know the statistics: about 44 percent of marriages in the United States end in divorce. About 40 percent of those who get divorced wind up remarrying, in addition to those who opt to live with a new partner or participate in some other, more flexible new family arrangement. Blended families have become part of the social fabric of our country, and each individual situation can give rise to a host of financial planning issues.

Such was the case with Sarah. She had been married to a successful businessman for many years, and since marrying, had never worked a day outside the home. As a traditional housewife, Sarah took care of the house, raised the children, and was completely absorbed with her role as wife and mother. So her world was completely rocked when, out of the blue, her husband announced one day that he wanted a divorce. After a fairly short legal process, during which Sarah and her soon-to-be-ex-husband relied mostly on his attorneys, a financial agreement was reached and their fiscal affairs were settled. Sarah then embarked on her new journey as a single person.

Unfortunately, it wasn't long before Sarah began encountering some financial problems. She had kept the family home as part of the divorce settlement, but the kids were grown and gone, and she had never considered how expensive it would be to maintain that big, empty house. She quickly realized that it was a money pit that she needed to get away from.

This isn't all that uncommon in divorce, as we saw in Chapter 8. When couples split, they often argue over who will get the house. But the one who wins that argument isn't always the winner in the end. That's because lot of people who go through divorce fail to analyze the true value of their resources. Even though various assets might have a particular fair market value on the "ledger," when it comes to asset division, there can be vastly different repercussions from coming away with assets that generate income, such as stocks and bonds, versus assets that are associated with future liabilities that will drain your money on a constant basis, such as a big house. Not only that, but when Sarah decided to sell the house, she hadn't counted on all the expenses associated with getting it in selling condition, such as sprucing up the landscaping and making repairs, not to mention the biggest selling expense of all: the real estate commission, which reduced her net proceeds by more than $30,000.

Another common mistake made when dividing assets during a divorce is to valuate a tax-deferred asset, such as an IRA or 401(k), as equivalent to the same amount of an after-tax investment account without considering the fact that you can't spend IRA money without paying tax on it first. As a practical matter, this means that tax-deferred assets should be discounted by a certain amount, say, 20 percent, before being compared directly to after-tax assets such as stocks, bonds, and mutual funds. If the tax effect is not taken into consideration, it's not an apples-to-apples comparison.

What's more, if the divorced spouse is under age 59½ and needs to withdraw money to live on from a tax-deferred asset, she will be subject not only to the ordinary income tax described above, but also to an additional 10 percent early withdrawal penalty. There is, however, an exception to this rule in cases involving 401(k) plans: If money is distributed directly out of one spouse's 401(k) pursuant to a Qualified Domestic Relations Order, the recipient can receive that money without being subject to the 10 percent penalty. This is one of the few instances in which this penalty can be avoided by a recipient who is under age 59½, and it can come in very handy in cases where the recipient spouse needs to spend some of the 401(k) money to live on right away. The divorced spouse can even take part of the 401(k) money that she's entitled to this way to avoid the penalty and move the rest into an IRA for future use.

Sarah had just assumed that she could comfortably live off the proceeds of the divorce settlement for the rest of her life, but neither she nor her divorce attorney had ever looked at the numbers closely (nor had she consulted a financial planner in advance of the divorce) in order to make sure that was actually the case. Turns out, she needed more money to live on than her portfolio could reasonably be expected to generate, which meant that if she wanted her money to last, she would have to get a job. This was something she had never even considered during the divorce process. She had never really worked in her life and didn't have any marketable skills. This added an entirely new and completely unexpected layer of stress and concern to her life.

In a lot of ways, people who expect to live off their portfolio after they're divorced face many of the same issues as people getting ready to retire—that is, they need to know how much they can withdraw each year from their nest egg and still have enough to last their entire lifetime. The answer depends on a range of factors, but, in general, most people need to follow what's called the "4 percent rule." If you need to take income every single year regardless of market conditions and you want to give yourself "inflation raises" or cost-of-living increases every year to maintain your purchasing power over time, you need to limit your yearly withdrawals to about 3 to 4 percent of the entire value of your nest egg. In recent years many advisors have become more cautious because of the current low interest rates, and are suggesting a lower withdrawal rate to help prevent running out of money. For example, if you want to live on $60,000 per year, you need to start out with a nest egg of about $1.5 million. In Sarah's case, that's about the level of yearly income that she needed, but unfortunately, her nest egg was less than half that size.

If Sarah had been older, another factor that most people don't know could have really helped her out: the Social Security divorced spouse benefit. With this little-known benefit, if you're divorced but were married for at least ten years, you are actually eligible to collect a Social Security benefit based on your ex-spouse's work record. (If you do have a work history of your own, you will receive this spousal benefit or your own Social Security benefit, whichever is higher.) This provision allows you to collect a benefit equal to one half of your ex-spouse's benefit, and that applies even if you never worked outside the home. This has no effect at all on your ex-spouse; he can still collect his own full Social Security benefit regardless of the fact that you're also collecting on his record. In order to qualify under this rule, you must be unmarried (i.e., divorced and not remarried), and both you and your ex-spouse must be at least 62 years old. The ex-spouse doesn't even have to be actually collecting his benefit, as long as he's at least 62 years old. If you wait to collect until your own normal retirement age (67 years old for most people), your benefit will be equal to one half of your ex-spouse's full retirement benefit. But you can begin to collect a reduced benefit as long as you're at least 62.

Unfortunately for Sarah, she was only in her early forties, so the Social Security divorced spouse benefit would not be available to help her for many years. So she struggled to find work and bounced from job to job for a while, and then wound up doing something else that far too many people do—rushing into another marriage without learning enough about her partner's financial history and habits.

There were red flags from the beginning. First of all, Mike was vague about his job. He told Sarah that he was an entrepreneur who would act as a CEO to bring a failing business back to profitability, and then move on to the next gig. In reality, he lived with his mother, in her house. This didn't worry Sarah because he explained that he was caring for his elderly mother who needed his help.

The next red flag was that Mike wanted them to get a house together—which Sarah would have to put up all the money to buy. He didn't have any money for a down payment, nor did he have good enough credit to qualify for any mortgage. He blamed his bad credit on problems caused by his ex-wife. Sarah would have to come up with the entire down payment, plus borrow all the money on her own, in order to purchase their new home.

This highlights an important principle: once you've been divorced (or widowed) and are considering getting remarried, it's important for both people in the relationship to clearly disclose to the other all their financial assets, liabilities, and income. It's also a good idea to share recent credit reports. Second marriages frequently fail because one spouse has massive debts that eventually surface and come as a complete shock and surprise to the other. Another reason behind failed marriages is that each spouse has different ideas about borrowing money and contributing to daily living expenses. It's important for any engaged couple to discuss these issues in advance, whether it's a first marriage or subsequent marriage. It's especially important later in life because there has been much more opportunity to accumulate debts and/or other financial problems along the way.

In Sarah's case, another red flag was that Mike was very aggressive about wanting to be added right away to the title of her investment account—the account that was comprised of the proceeds from her recent divorce. She wisely listened to financial advice and refrained from doing this, leaving her account in her name alone. In most states, property that you initially bring into a marriage is not considered divisible marital property in the event of divorce; rather, it's considered separate property. However, if you put your spouse's name on the title of any account, he could later make the argument that you intended to gift him half of the account and that it became marital property the day you added his name to the title. An ex-spouse might not necessarily win that argument, but he could try.

Everyone should give careful consideration as to how they title their assets, whether in a first or subsequent marriage. The way in which you title assets is always important and changes to titling can be significant, no matter when or why they are made. In addition, it's worth noting that comingling an asset can make it take on the nature of marital property. Comingling applies to any situation in which you retitle assets from your own name to any kind of joint account. For instance, comingling assets might include depositing one spouse's income into a joint account and using money from that account to buy other assets or property that is then jointly titled to both spouses. Such assets are considered marital property, and anything that is considered marital property is divisible in the event of divorce.

Unfortunately, Sarah ignored too many warning signs and went ahead with her second marriage. Fairly soon after the marriage, Mike "lost" his "job." Sarah noticed that he began drinking more heavily. He became more distant, and the marriage quickly went downhill. Before long, Sarah was looking at another divorce. And that's when yet another problem cropped up.

Sarah had bought the house they shared shortly after they were married. She had been careful to title the house in her name alone, since she had contributed the entire down payment, and she had taken out the mortgage on her own as well. The house was located in a neighborhood that was close to Mike's mother, but far away from Sarah's own parents and children. She wanted to sell the house and move elsewhere. However, in some states (including Ohio), any time one spouse acquires property during a marriage, the other spouse automatically gets "dower rights" in the property, regardless of who paid for it. (Dower rights refer to an arcane aspect of probate law.) This means that the owner can't sell the house unless her spouse signs off on his dower rights, even if the house is titled to the owner alone. These rights are extinguished once a divorce is final. Once Mike found out that Sarah couldn't sell her house without his signing off on it, he delayed the divorce to make the most of his bargaining leverage. He demanded a financial settlement from Sarah before he would agree to sign the divorce papers and sign off on his dower rights to her house. Of course, he was in no hurry to do so since he had no money of his own and nowhere else to go.

In the end, Sarah just had to grit her teeth and pay him off in order to be able to sell her house. It would have been smarter for her to heed the red flags in Mike's background and just rent for a while until she was sure the marriage was going to last, but she had followed her heart instead of her head, which, unfortunately, resulted in a costly lesson.

Sarah's case is just one example of how complicated issues regarding real estate can be when it comes to new relationships, regardless of whether those relationships lead to marriage. Even when both parties involved are financially sound, of good character, and have the best intentions, prickly issues can come out of nowhere.

This is exactly what happened to Steve and Edie. Both were in their late fifties, had been previously divorced, and came into the relationship owning their own houses. Even though they made a great couple and had been together in a solid relationship for more than a decade, they weren't legally married. Both of them had steady jobs and plenty of income, and after being together for many years, they decided to move in together. They planned to sell their houses and buy one together. Both of them would contribute half the down payment, and they would split the mortgage and other bills equally.

In their case, there was no real issue about the title to their new house: it would be jointly titled to both of them. The problem arose during the discussion of what would happen to the house if one of them passed away. If they broke up during their lifetimes, they could simply negotiate the point; the problem was that if one died before they split up, things could get tricky. It was this discussion about estate planning that raised red flags.

In any second marriage (or in this case, a "second relationship"), it's critically important to think about your estate planning issues and get your affairs in order. Where do you want your assets to go if something happens to you? To your new spouse or partner? Or, perhaps, to your children from a prior marriage? It's important to review the beneficiary designation forms for certain assets such as life insurance, annuities, IRAs, and 401(k)s to make sure these are properly updated. As long as the person you name on these forms outlives you, they will get that asset free and clear, with no probate. You can name primary beneficiaries and/or secondary beneficiaries, and even split the asset in percentages to more than one individual within the primary or secondary categories.

It's also important to review the title on all your financial accounts, such as savings or checking accounts at banks, CDs, stocks, savings bonds, and investment accounts. You could add someone as joint owner, which means that person would have immediate rights to that account, plus he would get that account upon your death with no probate. Or you could just make a transfer on death (TOD) or payable on death

(POD) designation on any given financial account, which allows the account to go to the named beneficiary upon your death with no probate, but doesn't give the beneficiary any rights to the account until that time.

In Steve and Edie's case, none of those methods would work. TOD/POD can go to anyone, and avoids probate, but it gives the property to the beneficiary free and clear. That wouldn't work in this case because neither Steve nor Edie wanted their halves of the house to pass free and clear to each other; they wanted it to pass to their own children, with a bunch of conditions attached.

Steve and Edie weren't intending to get married; they just wanted to own a house together. Both had children from their prior marriages, and they both agreed that if one of them passed away, neither wanted the decedent's half of the house to pass to the survivor. Instead, each wanted it to pass to the decedent's own children. How to assign survivor rights to the jointly owned house gave rise to a whole new level of complexity. It meant that they would have to use a trust.

The next issue to be decided was how much time should pass before the children would inherit their deceased parent's half of the house. Steve suggested a time frame of six months. As soon as Edie heard this, she burst into tears. "What are you saying?" she asked. "You'll have been gone only six months, and while I'd still be grieving over losing you, I'd be out of my home as well?" Edie was extremely upset at the thought of having to move out of their house so soon after Steve's death.

This proved to be a very difficult, and emotional, discussion. In the end they agreed to a time frame of eighteen months. Unfortunately, this was not the last of the tough decisions. Regardless of whether Steve or Edie died first, what if the survivor wanted the option to buy the other half of the house so he or she could continue living there? How much would the survivor have to pay the children for that half of the house? What if the survivor couldn't afford to buy out the children at that particular time?

The questions continued. How would the household possessions be divided? This was yet another contentious issue. They both initially thought that the survivor should keep the possessions he or she had brought into the house, and the decedent's things would go to his or her own children. That sounds reasonable enough, but exactly how would it be determined which possessions belonged to Steve and which to Edie? It might be easy enough to identify who brought the big screen TV over from their previous house, but what if they bought a new dining room set while they were living in the new house? Who did that belong to? This gave rise to a whole set of issues about which neither of them had given the slightest thought.

In essence, Steve and Edie were creating a plan for a property division, very much like what happens in divorce, except that the division of assets would follow the passing of one of them. In a case like this, a trust is often the best way to accomplish the desires of both parties. A trust allows the people forming it to create their own rules as to what happens to any property that's titled in the name of the trust. This is necessary when people want property to be governed by a variety of conditions, rather than just pass to someone outright.

Steve and Edie were eventually able to discuss all these issues, one by one, and come to a satisfactory resolution. Rules were written into the trust, and the new house was titled into the name of the trust rather than to Steve and Edie jointly. It was far from an easy process, but at least they had the foresight to carefully make their plans together, when the time was right and they were both healthy.

Not as lucky at romance was Janet. She, too, found herself divorced, but her next relationship didn't turn out as well as Steve's and Edie's. We'll look at Janet's story next, in Chapter 19.

Lessons Learned

- When dividing assets in a divorce, it's important to compare apples to apples, looking at the pros and cons of income-producing assets, such as stocks and bonds, as well as of assets that could become liabilities, such as real estate.
- When considering remarriage, be sure to investigate your betrothed's financial health, checking credit reports and looking at the status of all accounts, from checking and savings accounts to retirement accounts to investment portfolios.

123

- Whenever considering reassigning titles from your own name to a joint title, be sure you're comfortable with the fact that assets could be comingled, which might make for a messy untangling in the event of divorce.

CHAPTER 19

Break Up with Scammers

As we've seen, a change in circumstances can come as a surprise, followed by new situations that can be equally challenging. When it comes to relationships—and all the emotions involved—dealing with those changes can be tricky. Some of us can fall prey to the worst among us.

A growing percentage of women of a certain age are spending their preretirement and retirement years living alone. For many, this is a choice. For others, either the premature death of a spouse or an untimely or unexpected divorce may force them into a lifestyle they weren't necessarily planning for. Under such circumstances, it's natural to feel alone and to seek companionship with someone who is similarly situated. Dating is tough enough in the first place, and it can be especially difficult for those nearing retirement. Fortunately, with technological advances, finding a potential suitor isn't as hard as it may have been in the past.

Due to the introduction of a variety of mobile devices, we can use our smartphones not only to make and receive calls and text messages, but also to access the Internet from the palm of our hands. Singles can even use mobile apps on their phone to create profiles on various dating sites. This means that they can find their "perfect match" without utilizing the traditional methods, such as being set up by friends, visiting a favorite watering hole, or even meeting in the church choir. In many ways, the world seems much smaller and much less personal now than it did for previous generations. This can be both a blessing and a curse.

Technology has been a blessing for many people. Social networking sites such as Facebook allow us to easily reconnect with friends and former classmates we haven't been in contact with for years. In fact, the site will routinely suggest people we might know, thereby making it that much easier to make such a connection. Of course, Facebook is just one of the social media sites that connect us to people. Online dating sites like Match, eHarmony, and OurTime make finding friends and partners that much easier, too.[11] More and more stories are being told of couples who have found one another via the Internet, whether it was a new introduction or a reconnection from the past. By some measures, more than a third of marriages begin with online relationships.[12] The more we hear about stories like this, the more likely we are to believe that it can happen to us, too.

It can be easy to forget, however, that unintended consequences can arise from using such websites. For starters, these sites also give others access to you and, perhaps, to your personal information. Unfortunately, criminals aren't always recognizable when they're hiding behind a computer screen. Cyber criminals don't all wear masks and black trench coats. These days, they don't have to say, "This is a stick up" before they take your money. In fact, many end up stealing pictures of someone else and charming their victims by starting online relationships and feeding on the emotions of unsuspecting dates well before they begin the process of actually stealing anything.

This might seem unlikely, but it does happen—and more often than you might think. We don't necessarily hear from the victims because once they realize that they have been fooled, the embarrassment silences them, just as it did with Janet.

---

[11] Aaron Smith and Monica Anderson, "5 facts about online dating," PewResearch. org, April 20, 2015. Retrieved August 25, 2015 from http://www.pewresearch. org/fact-tank/2015/04/20/5-facts-about-online-dating/.

[12] Sharon Jayson, "Study: More than a third of new marriages start online," USAToday.com, June 3, 2013. Retrieved August 25, 2015, from http:// www.usatoday.com/story/news/nation/2013/06/03/online-dating-marriage/2377961/.

Janet had a close circle of female friends with whom she would communicate regularly. Her friends had a pretty good idea as to what was going on in her life. Many of these friends were married and had their own families to occupy much of their time. As a divorcée in her fifties with no children, Janet often felt lonely. For periods at a time, she seemed to vanish from her friends. They'd leave voicemails but would get no response.

Out of the blue one day, Janet called the group and asked if they could all get together for lunch. She said she had exciting news for them and wanted to share it in person. They set up a lunch, and each was looking forward to hearing her good news.

Janet was the first to arrive for the lunch and was beaming as each of her friends arrived. Each thought they'd never seen her look so happy. After they all were seated, she immediately announced she was getting married. Everyone was shocked. After all, none of them even knew she was dating someone, let alone in a serious relationship. She told them that her new fiancé was a master sergeant in the army, stationed in Afghanistan. He was 63 years old and a widower. His wife had died from breast cancer five years earlier. In addition, he had adopted a child from Ghana while he was there on a peacekeeping mission.

Still in a state of shock, her friends gradually started asking questions. One friend, who was a military spouse, asked if Janet was sure that her fiancé was 63 years old because she had never heard of a master sergeant who was that old. Another friend asked where his son was currently residing while he was in Afghanistan. She told the group that the child was back in Ghana staying with family. It struck them as more than a little odd that someone would adopt a child during a peacekeeping mission only to send the child back to the country from which the child was rescued. They wondered if better, more practical, arrangements could have been made. One friend questioned whether Janet's fiancé had any family or friends in the United States with whom the child could stay, but Janet couldn't answer the question.

And, then, Janet's sister asked how Janet had met her new man. She responded, proudly, that she was on a dating site and a random message popped up and they started chatting. Evidently, it was love at first keystroke. He said all of the right things, was well travelled, and quite successful. He was so successful, in fact, that he was able to make a fortune speculating on gold, in addition to serving our country proudly as a master sergeant.

Janet's circle of friends was almost at a loss for words, but they had a few more questions left in them. A friend asked her if she had given her new fiancé any money. Janet informed her that she had "invested" $25,000 in gold with him earlier in the week. To do so, she wired the funds to the Bank of Ghana. Moreover, she said, she was excited about the investment and was considering investing more. In her mind, she was likely to strike it rich.

Janet provided the group with her fiancé's name and email address, in the event that any of them had questions that they wanted to ask him directly. At the table, one of her friends used a cell phone to do a search on Facebook and pulled up a picture and asked if it was a picture of her "fiancé." She confirmed that it was. One by one, Janet's circle of friends became quite concerned for her. For starters, the picture looked like that of a 35-year-old, not a 63-year-old. And, he only had seven friends on Facebook, all of whom were women in their fifties. Her sister finally had to tell her that it was a scam. Janet was crushed. She was advised to contact the FBI and her bank to see if the funds could be rerouted.

Sadly, Janet has yet to receive any of her money back, whether from the bank or as a result of her "investment." And as her friends expected, shortly after the transfer of funds, her "fiancé" disappeared.

The moral of the story: If you ever receive an unsolicited message via the Internet, be careful. A popular, though not an exclusive, theme for these criminals is that of the American patriot serving our country while deployed overseas. If someone were to send a random message out of the blue, the recipient would probably delete it and think nothing of it. But, when told that the sender is off fighting on behalf of our country and that they are alone in a part of the world that neither wants nor understands them, we seem to follow our heart and completely disregard what our head is telling us.

Some criminals are very intelligent. They won't send you a message and immediately ask for money. They'll develop a relationship with you, saying all of the right things. At some point, relatively soon in the "relationship," they'll remark about how it seems that the two of you were meant to be together. Then, soon after, they'll come up with a financial crisis and "reluctantly" seek your help. When they do ask for financial help, they have a perfect excuse as to why the money needs to be wired to Africa or directly into a bank account in a country with far fewer banking regulations than those in the Unites States. Be advised: Nearly all of these "cries for help" are scams.

Unfortunately, romance scams are becoming more prevalent. Romance scammers often target men and women who live alone, whether through widowhood or divorce. According to the U.S. Department of State, "The amounts lost by U.S. citizens in these types of scams can range from relatively small amounts to more than $400,000."[13] A recent study found that "According to the National Consumers League (NCL), the average victim of a 'sweetheart swindle' lost more than $3,000 in 2007" and that "online dating fraud was one of the most commonly reported complaints in the ever- rising internet fraud claims."[14]

Websites such as RomanceScams.org track scams perpetrated against innocent people. These might be helpful if you or someone you know suspect a romance scam. But in the meantime, be wary of getting involved with someone you can't actually meet in person or at least speak to over the phone. If someone can't tell you where he is located because he's on a secret mission that is critical to national security, then he has no business being on a social media site in the first place. And, most important, never wire money outside of the country, especially to countries in Africa.

If you think that you might be in a situation in which you are being victimized, do your research. Before sending any money or personal data, discuss the situation with your friends, CPA, financial advisor, or local law enforcement. Be honest, with both yourself and your support

---

[13] U.S. Department of State, "Internet Dating and Romance Scams," Travel.State. gov, n.d. Retrieved August 25, 2015, from http://travel.state.gov/content/ passports/english/emergencies/scams/dating.html.

[14] Aunshul Rege. "What's Love Got to Do with It? Exploring Online Dating Scams and Identity Fraud," *International Journal of Cyber Criminology*, July–December 2009, Vol. 3(2), p. 495. Retrieved August 17, 2015, from http://www.cybercrimejournal.com/AunshulIJCCJuly2009.pdf.

network, because it is extremely difficult to recover funds that have already been sent.

Lessons Learned

- Romance scams are becoming more prevalent, with the average victim losing about $3,000 and some victims losing more than $400,000.
- Romance scammers tend to target widows and widowers, divorcees, and retirees who live alone.
- Be careful about sharing personal information online. Don't post online any information that might be subject to identity fraud or that might provide a romance scammer with ammunition to trick you into giving away your savings.

Part III

Manage Your Future— Which Begins Now

If we've planned ahead and saved wisely, we should be able to retire well. After years of saving, managing debt, investing carefully, and planning for healthcare expenses and long-term care needs, we've come to the point where it's time to put our plans into action.

During our retirement years, we shift from accumulating wealth for retirement to now having those assets generate monthly retirement income. Much of this requires ongoing risk management as we face the need to make our nest eggs last for ten or twenty years—or even longer.

CHAPTER 20

Shift to Risk Management

From an investment management perspective, the years preceding retirement can be difficult to navigate. Many of our working years are spent accumulating assets in preparation for the day on which we stop receiving a paycheck from our employer. Upon retirement, we enter into the distribution phase with regard to our assets. During the distribution phase, it's not uncommon to see a decrease in retirement assets, depending upon both the amount we are withdrawing in order to maintain a standard of living and the rate of return on the underlying assets.

Psychologically, this can be troublesome for retirees, and they often tend to start viewing risk differently. While working, employees often downplay the risk in their portfolios because they think they have plenty of time to recover from potential market downturns. With proper planning, they can forecast how much they should be setting aside in order to supplement the retirement income they'll likely receive from Social Security. They can even factor in several different rates of return and come up with an annual contribution that is comfortable for them to make.

Once retired, however, retirees are more concerned about not depleting their retirement savings. They view risk as a threat to their nest egg. Even the slightest correction in the market can lead to panic because they are no longer making sizable contributions to their investments each year. In short, if their assets diminish, they have less from which to draw their retirement income.

It can be easy to disregard the necessity to view risk differently when retirement approaches. Investment decisions made when we were in our forties can look fantastic at age 65. We see twenty years of growth in a portfolio and are tempted to assume that the next twenty years will be just as prosperous. In doing so, it can be easy to forget difficult economic times in which investments were down 20 or 30 percent or even worse. For example, the tech bubble of the late 1990s or the mortgage crisis of the early 2000s might not appear as significant today because portfolios eventually emerged seemingly unscathed. However, consider that portfolio holders who were in the distribution phase of their assets during those times likely had a different view. This lack of hindsight can, at times, lead us to focus on chasing a greater return on our investments instead of protecting what we've earned.

The need to balance risk and reward can be forgotten at the most inopportune times. When transitioning into retirement, we may fail to adjust our expectations for our investment portfolios to reflect a new outlook on risk. The consequences may ultimately involve having to continue working well beyond a desired retirement age or to scale back a retirement lifestyle. Consider the story of Jodi and Michael.

Jodi and Michael were both 59 years old and were considering retiring in the next few years. They'd been married for twenty-three years and had raised Jodi's son from a previous marriage. Jodi worked in higher education as an adjunct faculty member, and Michael was employed by a consulting firm. For the previous ten years or so, together they earned "more money than they could spend," as Michael proudly reported. They were quite comfortable and had no debt and had even purchased their vehicles with cash. They were never in a position in which they had to worry about money. In fact, Michael would often leave his paychecks on the dresser for months at a time because he forgot to deposit them in the bank and he had never bothered setting up a direct-deposit account. They were looking forward to spending their retirement years at home while embarking on one or two global vacations each year.

From a financial standpoint, Jodi and Michael felt that they had no reason to believe that their goals weren't achievable. Just to be sure, though, they sought a second opinion from a financial advisor.

They revealed to the advisor that they desired a retirement income of $90,000 each year beginning when they were both 65 years old. Of that, $40,000 would be devoted annually to travel. They also indicated that they would like to purchase a new car every four to five years. Aside from the travel and the cars, their expenses would be nominal. Both would have access to retiree health insurance through their employers, which would supplement Medicare for a reasonable cost. In addition, there was no mortgage on their house. They did like to eat their meals away from home, and that would be part of their daily living expenses. Their home was beautifully furnished, and they looked forward items to continuing buying quality items for their home.

Jodi and Michael enjoyed spending money, but they were also good at saving it. They had nearly $100,000 in a savings account, and nearly $2 million in various retirement and individual investment accounts. Michael had experienced some health issues at one point, and going through that had encouraged the couple to do their estate planning. To avoid the probate process, they had each set up revocable trusts into which they transferred individually owned assets and designated the trusts as the beneficiary of their retirement accounts. Overall, Jodi and Michael had done a thorough job of planning for their retirement. But there was one glaring weakness in their plan.

Before joining a small consulting firm, Michael had spent thirty years working for a large multinational corporation. As a benefit of this employment, Michael was able to purchase this company's stock at a discount and he was able buy the stock within his 401(k). Michael did just that, and he did so aggressively. For many years, the company had performed quite well, and Michael's investment in the company had grown to more than $1 million.

But this one holding represented more than half of their investable assets. There was simply too much risk in their portfolio due to such a concentrated position. Jodi and Michael agreed that it was risky to have so much of their net worth tied into one company, but they neglected to take action because the company was so well respected and the stock had performed so well throughout the years during which they owned it. Michael indicated that they would liquidate the position in a few years as they got closer to retirement. In doing so, Michael thought, it would give them a few more years of significant growth, which would further enhance their retirement lifestyle.

Within sixteen months after their initial meeting, Jodi and Michael experienced the unthinkable. Michael had not taken action to reduce their ownership in his former employer's stock, and the stock had subsequently plummeted by 75 percent. Worse yet, many lines of business within the company were sold off, and revenue projections were not favorable for a return to the previous value of the stock. As such, Jodi's and Michael's liquid assets were cut nearly in half when they were just two years away from retirement. For the first time in ages, they were forced to worry about their retirement lifestyle. Moreover, they were concerned that they wouldn't be able to retire at age 65.

Jodi and Michael suddenly became risk averse and, initially, wanted to put all their money into "safe" investments. Simply put, they were shell-shocked. But this new, overly cautious approach wasn't practical. Without any growth in their portfolio, their retirement income could be jeopardized by inflation. If the return on investment did not at least meet what they were withdrawing plus the increases in their cost of living, it would be unlikely that their nest egg could sustain them long into retirement. After carefully discussing it with an advisor, they settled on a well-diversified portfolio. While diversifying their assets certainly couldn't prevent any future losses, they should be able to better survive any dramatic stock market drops in the future. This more thoughtful approach seemed to reduce the stress they were experiencing with their investments.

Three years after reallocating their portfolio and viewing their investment risk in a different light, Jodi and Michael were able to regain roughly 60 percent of what was lost. Had they not diversified after the correction and remained overly cautious, they probably would have recouped even less.

Their nest egg is still significantly smaller than it was once, but they both were still able to retire at the age of 65. Their income is comparable to what they were expecting. The reason for this is that, after recognizing the loss in the stock, Jodi and Michael started saving more of their earnings and contributed a greater percentage to their respective 401(k)s. Suffering the loss while they were still accumulating assets enabled them to mitigate some of the damage. They have, however, changed certain things about their lifestyle. Instead of purchasing a new car every four to five years, they have extended it to every six to seven years. They do not eat out at restaurants as much, and they are reluctant to spend as freely on items for the home. The result of these lifestyle changes is that they can afford to do what they really wanted to do in retirement, which is travel.

Jodi and Michael were lucky. Had the loss of value in the stock occurred after they retired, it would have been virtually impossible to maintain the standard of living to which they were accustomed. In fact, there is a good chance that one of them would have been forced to reenter the workforce after retiring. This would not have been the result that they had envisioned after years spent planning so carefully for their retirement. By going through this crisis, they learned valuable lessons about risk: it can come from the most unexpected of places.

In managing risk, what happens when a couple has different risk tolerances, or when the financial manager in the family becomes ill and passes away? We'll look at those scenarios, in Chapter 21.

Lessons Learned

- Part of financial planning includes managing risk and rebalancing portfolios as retirement draws nearer. Careful consideration should be given to moving some of your more aggressive holdings to more conservative ones in an attempt to reduce the volatility in your portfolio.
- It can be financially disastrous to invest heavily in any single asset. What might look like a hot stock today could be a loser tomorrow, and even the savviest investors can be surprised by sudden market downturns. Be sure to allocate your investments across a broad range of stocks, bonds, real estate, and insurance in order to cover all your bases in retirement.

- Successful retirement planning requires that you frequently and regularly revisit your plan and your portfolio, making sure that everything is performing and proceeding as planned and, if not, reallocating as necessary in order to preserve and protect the retirement lifestyle you desire.

CHAPTER 21

Prior Planning Prevents Poor Performance

Investing for the retiree is, in many ways, about taking calculated risks. As we approach and enter our retirement years, we have to balance the type of return we hope to achieve with the amount we are willing to lose in order to achieve it.

Some of us can do this by ourselves, but others may need a little help in the process.

Some people have too many other things they want do with their time and simply don't think a fulfilling way to spend it is by analyzing investment options, cash flow analyses, and research reports. Or, they've never really handled the finances in their household and don't want to start doing so once they've retired.

There are those, however, who get a rush of adrenaline by taking control of their investments. They're fascinated by the research and create a challenge for themselves, such as outperforming a benchmark (e.g., the S&P 500 or the Russell 2000) or one that they have customized themselves. They might be looking for the next value stock out there, one that has fallen in terms of valuation but is poised to make a comeback. These individuals might be constantly logging on to their computer to see where their portfolio stands and devouring every bit of financial news out there. In short, they are risk takers, and investing becomes their retirement hobby.

It's not uncommon to see two-person households representing each of these respective categories. This blend of the two personalities can complement their retirement planning strategy just as it has complemented their marriage for many years. While one is researching investments for the portfolio, the other may be out working in the yard or engaging in another hobby. One might suggest taking on more investment risk and the other, although not too concerned about the actual details, might voice concern about the impact that a loss could have on their lifestyle. The result could be the assumption of some risk, but perhaps not as much as initially proposed. This partnership can serve many couples well.

Problems arise, however, when one of the partners is not able to complete the "role" he or she has assumed. If, for example, the financial manager of the family becomes ill or passes away, then daily attention to the portfolio might be lacking and regular needed adjustments might not be made. Conversely, if the "voice of reason" is no longer providing insight, then the investment decisions might become overly aggressive, incurring more risk than desirable. As is with many things in life, this balance is critical to prospering. In such cases, when the balance is thrown off, it is best to seek counsel from someone who can help restore it.

Richard and Joan provide an example of this. They were what many would consider to be the perfect couple, married for more than fifty years with three grown children. Their children were all quite successful, and although each lived over a day's drive from their parents, the family remained close.

Richard was a chemical engineer and was detail oriented by nature. He had enjoyed many years as a senior-level executive with several large chemical companies. Richard was in charge of the family's finances, and he handled their investments with same degree of precision that he utilized in his professional life. When Richard wasn't working, or he and Joan weren't attending the orchestra, enjoying other arts, or vacationing to see their children, he was consumed by financial data. He would frequently buy and sell various equities, and his portfolio contained a rather significant degree of risk. Though a risk taker, he was quite successful in building their wealth.

Joan, on the other hand, hated to deal with finances. She was the primary caregiver as their children were growing up, and she ran the household. She had a checking account, but it usually was funded with just enough for her to spend on groceries and other miscellaneous expenses. She enjoyed cooking, the arts, and working in her garden. It was fulfilling for her to nurture her plants so that something was always in bloom and there were fresh vegetables to enhance her culinary efforts.

Richard and Joan retired at the age of 62, having accumulated a significant nest egg. Their liquid assets were in excess of $3 million. In addition, their home was unencumbered. Their retirement income was near six figures a year, and there really was little reason for them to worry about the sustainability of their assets.

Like Jodi and Michael in the previous section, they sought the counsel of an estate planning attorney to ensure that there would be a seamless and tax-efficient transfer of assets upon the death of each of them. In doing so, they each created a revocable trust and transferred a significant portion of their assets into their respective trusts.

A revocable trust is designed to have earned income distributed by the grantor, who can alter or cancel any provisions of the trust. After death, the property in the trust transfers to beneficiaries.

When Richard and Joan reached their mid-seventies, it became clear to them that their home was no longer going to be a viable long-term place for them to live, so they purchased an apartment that was being built in a nearby retirement community. The cost was significant, but it would be a practical home for them in their advancing years. They would be living independently while still having ready access to assisted living and full nursing care within the same facility, should they need it. They also would have access to a dining facility and a shuttle service that would take them virtually anywhere they wanted to go, including the orchestra. Most important to them was the fact that none of their children would be burdened with the obligation to care for either or both of them should their health decline. After all, they wanted their children to visit and enjoy their time with them, not care for them.

Prior to the construction of their new housing being complete, Richard became seriously ill and passed away shortly thereafter. Joan was devastated. Not only had she lost her best friend and partner of more than fifty years, but now she had to manage their personal finances, which she had never done. In fact, she really didn't even have a true grasp on how much money they had or how long it might sustain her. None of her children was well versed in investments, so Joan met with her estate planning attorney for his suggestion on a qualified financial advisor.

Upon reviewing their portfolio, Joan was amazed with how well Richard had managed their assets and was able to see that her trust assets alone would be able to sustain her in retirement. She was receiving Social Security and would need nearly $4,000 each month to pay the fees associated with the retirement community where she would be residing. Her unit became available, and so she quickly sold her home and moved into the apartment that she and Richard had purchased, even though she would now be living alone.

Now that she would be handling the finances on her own, and not being a risk taker, Joan wanted her portfolio to be somewhat conservative. She preferred tax-free municipal bonds and other income-producing asset classes over the equity investments that Richard had favored. Her advisor was able to help her create a portfolio that would meet her income needs and outpace reasonable inflation without assuming more risk than she was comfortable with. Best of all for Joan was that a certain amount would be transferred to her checking account each month from which to pay her bills. If she needed more, whether to make a gift or buy orchestra tickets, all she had to do was call the advisor and she would have the funds within days. The simplicity of this approach put Joan at ease.

As for Richard's trust assets, Joan was the beneficiary during her lifetime and, upon her death, the assets would pass to their children. Joan felt confident that she would not need to take distributions from this trust, but she was reassured knowing that the assets would be there if she needed them. The fact that she had earmarked these assets for their children gave Joan the freedom to use her trust assets for herself as she saw fit. In other words, Joan had no reason to feel guilty about spending money on herself, and her quality of life would not be hindered.

When Joan sold the couple's home, she had a significant inflow of cash without a real need for it. The estate plan provided for assets to pass to their children upon the death of the survivor, but it really didn't immediately provide anything for anyone other than Joan. Knowing that she was well situated financially, Joan wanted to make gifts to her children and grandchildren. In her mind, she might live another twenty years, and if she could assist them with immediate needs, rather than making them wait until her death to receive anything, then she would prefer to do that. As such, she made a gift of cash to each of her children, and she created Section 529 college savings plans for each of her grandchildren. These gifts relieved considerable financial burdens for each of the recipients. Best of all, Joan was able to see the gifts put to good use and experience the moment with each of them as they received the gifts over the holidays. For Joan, this was far better than a transfer upon her death. Joan's children, though not financially strapped, were grateful. Her grandchildren, some too young to appreciate the magnitude of the gift, will feel blessed when they graduate from college without significant debt.

Joan has been able to thrive in retirement. Richard's trust, much like Richard himself, takes on the risks that Joan would not be completely comfortable with if it was her sole source of support. Her trust assets, on the other hand, are far more conservative and provide a stream of income that is necessary for her to maintain her standard of living. Either of these on their own may not be sufficient to accomplish each of the objectives that Richard and Joan had established years ago. Collectively, the balance created by the differing portfolios has provided the solution that Joan was in search of upon Richard's death.

There are many reasons to use a trust as part of an estate plan, but not every situation calls for one, which is why we'll discuss how and why to incorporate trusts into your overall planning, in Chapter 22.

Lessons Learned

- Long-term planning should incorporate a strategy for dealing with the premature death of the family's financial manager.

- A revocable trust can be a useful tool in structuring assets for disbursement while mitigating estate taxes.
- In addition to or in lieu of providing inheritances for survivors, retirees could also plan for gifting assets to their children and grandchildren during their lifetime.

CHAPTER 22

Put Your Faith in Trusts

Developing and implementing a successful comprehensive financial plan isn't necessarily an easy task. Many different moving parts have to be coordinated to effectively manage your overall financial affairs. By the time people take care of issues related to their daily lives, such as managing the house, the job, and the kids, little time or energy is left to figure out how to set up their financial accounts and manage their investments. Unfortunately, one of the most important issues that often falls by the wayside is estate planning.

The term "estate planning" tends to evoke thoughts of managing large mansions and trust funds, but it actually is a concept that applies to everyone. Estate planning is not just for the wealthy; it's for anyone who owns anything. It means making sure that your assets go to the people that you truly care about, at the right time, and in the right amounts, hopefully while minimizing taxes and avoiding probate at the same time. Not unlike how Richard planned to provide for Joan and their children, in Chapter 21, estate plans tackle specifically how assets are passed to heirs and survivors. If there is a bank account, an IRA, real estate, or any asset you would like to protect and preserve, then an estate plan is called for. Anyone who wishes to save the family from the struggle of cleaning up the piles of paperwork left after the passing of a loved one should create an estate plan. Indeed, some might argue that the moment you begin saving money, you have begun your estate planning.

Trusts can be one of your most valuable tools when setting up your estate plan, perhaps even essential to achieving your goals. Trusts are just one way to provide for survivors, such as Richard did for Joan, and they are an important consideration when creating your will and preserving your legacy.

However, many people have common misconceptions about why they might need a trust, what a trust can really do for them, and whether they even need one at all. When people have a trust, it is typically put on a shelf somewhere to gather dust and many times is forgotten. Even if they do remember they have a trust, it's a big mystery as to what it says, and oftentimes they forget why they had it done in the first place. So, why would someone need a trust?

Let's first explain what we mean when we use the term "trust." A living trust (sometimes called an "inter vivos" or "revocable" trust) is a written legal document through which your assets are held by a trustee for your benefit during your lifetime and then transferred to designated beneficiaries at your death by your chosen representative, called a "successor trustee." Usually a husband and wife (known as the "grantors") create a joint trust, such as Richard and Joan did, which they manage as co-trustees during their joint lifetimes for their mutual benefit. When one spouse becomes incapacitated or passes away, the other carries on as sole trustee for the rest of his or her life. The grantors usually keep total control of the assets along the way, meaning that they have the right to amend and/or terminate the entire arrangement until at least the death of the first spouse. And once the second spouse passes away, the assets typically go to the children, with the advantage of avoiding probate.

A lot of people really get hung up on that last issue—avoiding probate. It's certainly true that avoiding probate is usually a good idea. After all, probate often ties up assets for prolonged periods of time, in addition to being time consuming, burdensome, and often expensive. And it's also true that assets placed into a trust will completely avoid probate, which is a good thing. In fact, when most people are asked why they already have a trust, or why they think they might need one, they almost always answer by saying that it's to avoid probate.

But here's an interesting fact that most people don't realize. It turns out that you do not actually need a trust in order to avoid probate, in most cases. The fact is that there are lots of other easier, inexpensive ways to avoid probate, ways that are much simpler than using a trust. For example, when real estate is titled as joint tenancy with survivorship, when one owner dies, the property passes to the survivor with no probate. This is often the best solution for a married couple. If you think this form of titling would work for your situation, the key is to check for the proper language on your house title. If you can't locate the title, it can be obtained from your local real estate recorder's office.

For people who are unmarried, a better option might be to use what's called a transfer-on-death (TOD) title. The property will pass to whomever the owner names as TOD beneficiaries, with no probate. The difference between the two is that with a TOD title, the owner is not giving up any ownership rights to the property while they're alive; they are just naming beneficiaries to take the property without probate upon their death. On the other hand, joint tenancy with survivorship gives the joint owner immediate and equal ownership rights to the entire property.

It's also important to note that joint tenancy with survivorship, and/or TOD titling, can be used not only with real estate, but also with financial accounts such as investments, stocks, bonds, savings accounts, certificates of deposit, and so on. Any account that is in an individual's name can be re-titled either as joint tenancy with survivorship and/or TOD. If the owner does this, then upon their passing the entire account(s) will pass with no probate whatsoever.

There are other economical and straightforward ways to avoid probate. Many types of accounts have what are called "beneficiary designation forms." These would include things like IRAs, 401(k)s, life insurance policies, and annuities. If the owner of one of these accounts dies having named someone on the beneficiary form who outlives them, the beneficiary will take that account automatically, with no probate. Since many people have the vast majority of their financial wealth tied up in these types of accounts, you can see that the beneficiary designation forms are extremely important, and can be a very effective tool to make sure that nearly all of your wealth can pass outside of probate.

All of the techniques mentioned above are easy, low cost, and available to most people to make sure that the vast majority (if not all) of their assets pass outside of probate.

Let's take a moment to clear up yet another very common misconception. Many people think that they also need a trust to save on estate taxes. In simple terms, an estate tax is levied when the government valuates all your property after your death and finds the value exceeds a certain amount. The tax must be paid before the beneficiaries can get their share. The assessed value of your estate could include the appraised value of your real estate at your death, the fair market value of all your investments, the contents of bank and other financial accounts, and even any proceeds from life insurance policies.

In the early 1980s, anything in excess of $250,000 was considered an estate that was large enough to potentially be subject to federal estate taxes. Due to tax changes over the past few years, estates have to be worth more than $5 million before they are subject to any federal estate tax. For the vast majority of people, having an estate tax issue is now highly unlikely, so there is little reason to have a trust for that purpose.

So, if you don't need a trust to avoid probate, your estate is under the $5 million dollar threshold, and you won't have to worry about the estate tax, in what situation might you need to use a trust?

For the majority of families a trust may not be necessary, because for most of us the goal is to transfer our assets quickly and efficiently to our beneficiaries, free and clear, 100 percent under their own control for the rest of their lives. Once both parents are gone, and their children have grown up and become independent, there's no reason not to just have the assets pass straight to them and hope that they will make wise decisions for the rest of their lives. For these families, these typical probate avoidance techniques will work just fine.

But there are situations where you may want to have control of how your assets are distributed once you are deceased. What if one of the children has a mental or physical condition that makes it undesirable for them to directly inherit any assets? This could include a variety of situations such as a child with Down syndrome, a substance abuse problem, ora spouse the parents feel is overly controlling; someone facing bankruptcy; or a beneficiary who would be disqualified from certain government benefits/programs if they inherited money outright. Controlling how your assets are distributed can also come into play with second marriages that take place fairly late in life, where a parent wants to take care of that new spouse but doesn't necessarily want them to inherit all their assets outright. In cases like this, the person may feel that once they are gone, the assets will need to be managed by someone else for the beneficiary, rather than having the beneficiary just take full and immediate control over all the assets.

The legal term for this is "controlling assets from the grave." Maybe you want your beneficiary to have access to the income from your portfolio, but no more. Or you want to limit their rights to invade the principal to specified amounts or for special purposes—a business start-up, health expenses, a house purchase, or education. Maybe you even want to have the remaining principal go to charity upon the death of your beneficiaries. In cases like this, the only way to accomplish these goals is to use a trust. With a trust, the grantor is free to craft any language they want into the legal document, such that the money is controlled by whatever rules and conditions they see fit. And in situations like this, a trust can prove to be an indispensable tool to accomplish the grantor's objectives, making sure that the assets pass to the right people, at the right time, in the right amounts.

The bottom line is that proper estate planning is an essential component of every family's overall financial plan. Whatever the goals and objectives are, it's important to carefully examine all the tools that are available to make sure that your hard-earned assets are used to their fullest advantage to help the family members that you care about.

Changes in tax laws over the past several decades have minimized some of the concern individuals used to have for saving on estate taxes and minimizing probate, but there are still plenty of issues related to estate planning that need attention, which we will discuss in Chapter 23.

Lessons Learned

- Most people have misconceptions about what trusts are and what they can do for you. If the goal is just to avoid probate, there are many "cheap and easy" ways to get that done without needing a trust.

- Due to recent changes in the estate tax law, most families with estates valued at under $5 million should never have to pay federal estate taxes and thus don't need a trust for that purpose.
- There are many situations where a trust can be an essential tool, often involving instances where someone wants to "control their assets from the grave" by specifying the conditions and/or timing under which their beneficiaries ultimately benefit from the assets.

CHAPTER 23

Cover Your Assets

Even though the majority of the people in the United States don't have to worry about paying any federal estate transfer taxes at their death, there are still concerns related to income taxes, specifically to taxes assessed on distributions from IRAs and annuities.

Assets such as annuities are used to defer taxes on interest earned until the interest is withdrawn, or spent. Annuities are insurance company products designed to provide guaranteed lifetime income to the annuitant, or policyholder. While the annuity, as an asset, might not be subject to an estate tax, the income distributed from that annuity through the estate will result in taxable income. Spouses have an option to continue to defer the income from an annuity tax-free, but if the beneficiary is the estate, trust, or individual who is not a spouse, then the deferred income will be reported and is eligible to be taxed.

Annuity contracts are a good way to control income taxes, but they can create some income tax issues for beneficiaries other than a spouse. Much like an IRA, most insurance companies allow a surviving spouse who is named the primary beneficiary to receive the contract and maintain deferral of income until the time of his or her subsequent death.

Here's an example of how that might work. Larry and Lucy have been married for more than thirty years. During the course of their marriage, they were able to save a significant amount of money. But Larry lamented every year at tax time about the extra taxes being paid on the interest earned on his savings. He investigated an annuity and learned that he could earn interest but not have it reported on his tax returns every year. So several years ago, he decided to put $50,000 into a tax-deferred annuity. He had no immediate need for the interest it earned, and he didn't want to pay income taxes if he could avoid it for now, so a tax-deferred annuity made sense.

Lucy was named the primary beneficiary of the annuity. A feature commonly offered with an annuity is that, upon the death of the original annuitant (Larry in this case), the designated beneficiary can become the new owner and annuitant and maintain the original deferral and benefit. That means that, in this situation, Lucy would be afforded the same tax-deferred annuity and related benefits that Larry enjoyed while he was alive. This is not always the case: Under most annuity contracts available today, a beneficiary other than a spouse will receive the settlement and have to pay taxes on the income deferred in excess of principal. Nonspousal beneficiaries such as a child, sibling, or other natural person will pay taxes on the deferred interest on a pro rata basis when the death claim is settled and the funds are distributed to the named beneficiaries. If no beneficiary is named, then the estate becomes the beneficiary and a probate will be opened to distribute according to the will of the decedent. Because of this, it's important to make sure your beneficiaries are current on all your paperwork.

In addition to deferring taxes, estate planning also seeks to minimize taxes as well as any transfer and distribution costs. An annuity is useful in that probate will be avoided with a named beneficiary (although income taxes remain an issue). There may be no federal or state taxes with which to contend, but the beneficiaries will have to report their share of deferred income when the death benefit is claimed.

Moving an asset out of the estate can be helpful, but avoiding income taxes for the beneficiaries also is important. There is a way for beneficiaries to avoid having taxable income coming from the estate.

Let's say for the point of discussion that there is a deferred annuity owned in Paul's name. Paul is the annuitant, and his wife, Mary, is the beneficiary. Paul and Mary had begun accumulating money in annuities years ago, largely as a way to preserve tax-deferred income. Paul and Mary have two children, Ray and Robert, and saving income taxes now and later is important to all of them. Paul's annuity is worth $600,000 with deferred income of $400,000. Paul predeceased Mary by several years, and she still wasn't spending the interest income being deferred in the annuity. Ray and Robert stand to inherit the annuity because as contingent beneficiaries, Mary made clear the desire to try to pass the $600,000 value to the children and have no income taxes paid by them. With Mary's estate being less than $5 million, there will be no federal or state death taxes in this particular situation.

So how could Paul and Mary bestow an annuity to their children on a tax-free basis? Three things have to happen: create an irrevocable life insurance trust (ILIT), annuitize, and obtain life insurance.

First, with the assistance of an estate planning attorney, an ILIT was created and a request was made for an employer identification number (EIN) for the trust. An ILIT refers to any asset in the trust that is not owned by the individual (i.e., the grantor) who created the trust. Because the trust is its own entity, an EIN was needed.

The second step was for the couple to apply for a life insurance policy that covers both of them but pays only upon the second death, otherwise known as a second-to-die, last-to-die, or survivorship policy. Paul and Mary made a trial application for the policy and went through the normal underwriting, which would include a medical history, doctors' reports, and anything else deemed necessary by the insurance company. Paul and Mary made a trial application as the owners of the policy and the insureds. Once approval was obtained on the life insurance application, the trust then made application by formally requesting to be both the owner and the beneficiary of the life insurance policy on Paul and Mary, who remain the insureds. Insurance companies familiar with this process will then close out the file for the original application and replace it with a new application using the same insureds but stipulating the new EIN of the trust as owner.

Then application was made to the existing annuity, which is put into a payout mode known as annuitizing. Annuitizing is what happens when the insurance company begins sending checks for the lifetime of the annuitant, in this case Paul. This process guarantees that Paul will never run out of money on this particular annuity. Once the payments begin, there will be a distribution, usually annually. Part of the annuity payment is return of principal, and part is income. The income is taxable, and taxes are typically withheld for the convenience of the annuitant.

Finally, Paul used the proceeds from the annuity to make an annual gift to the ILIT. Because this gift is going to the trust and because the children are giving up the right to receive the money as a gift, the children have to waive their rights in order to allow the money to get put into the trust. By doing that, Ray and Robert preserve the plan to have an otherwise income-taxed asset (i.e., the annuity) pass to the children through the trust in the form of tax-free life insurance proceeds.

In order for this process to work successfully, at least one of the applicants, in this case either Paul or Mary, must be insurable so that a life insurance policy can be issued on one of them.

If for some reason the couple is not insurable, this process won't work as described. Because the policy doesn't pay until the second death, the underwriting usually allows for a survivorship/last-to-die policy to be issued, when a single life policy might have been rejected.

Either way, the trust will own the insurance policy, and the trust is the beneficiary of the policy. The terms of the trust will determine how the trust assets will be distributed according to the wishes of the grantor at the time of the creation of the trust. Trust assets would most likely consist of the insurance policy only, but the grantor is not prevented from including any asset deemed suitable. Other assets such as cash, for instance, may be donated to the ILIT, but a life insurance policy is the most common instrument used in such cases.

For Paul and Mary, the insurance premiums were to be paid from the proceeds of the annuity. Once the annuity contract was put into annuity mode, a regular stream of income would be paid to the owner/ annuitant for a specified period of time, usually lifetime. The annuitant then uses the money received from the annuity to pay the premium on the life insurance policy.

What typically happens is that a gift is made to the children and then, procedurally, the children decline the gift; the trust then uses the money to pay the premiums on the life insurance. Because this is an ILIT, the assets are removed from the estate of the decedent, and the children, as the trust's beneficiaries, receive the life insurance proceeds when both insureds have died. Life insurance benefits are income tax free and, because the trust is outside the estate, the estate tax would be avoided as well. So Raymond and Robert now have an inheritance on which no estate or income taxes will be paid.

In essence, Paul and Mary have chosen to accept the income on the annuity today, make an annual gift of the after-tax portion of the annuity income to their children, remove an asset from Paul's estate, and provide his children with income tax–free proceeds.

While this situation demonstrates how life insurance can be used to solve a need, the need for life insurance doesn't necessarily go away just because the children are grown and the mortgage is paid off. There are other benefits of life insurance policies.

Life insurance also can help build an estate or legacy. Scott, for example, wanted to leave his family some additional security. He did not accumulate money in an IRA or 401(k), and his modest house was still mortgaged to pay for the college loans for his two children. He still wished to create an estate for his family. Scott decided to use dollars to purchase a life insurance policy. This way he would be able to leave behind a sum of money greater than the accumulated premiums he paid. The death benefits would pass income tax-free to his beneficiaries, so he could accomplish a tax-free transfer of wealth.

If your health is good enough, life insurance companies may approve underwriting you even at a more advanced age and, sometimes, despite previous health conditions such as heart attack or stroke. Underwriting standards today acknowledge that people are living longer and that people are living more healthy lifestyles with reduced tobacco use, more exercise, better diets, and improved medical care.

Life insurance provides the opportunity to leave loved ones or dependents a gift that you otherwise might not have been able to do. Life insurance could be the reason that your family becomes mortgage free or debt free. The proceeds from a policy could provide money to pay for a college education or start-up funds to launch a business venture. While creating a source of money that is income tax free to the beneficiary, a life insurance policy also might serve as a way for the insured to accumulate money and provide a hedge against potential creditors. Some beneficiaries struggle with money problems, which can be alleviated by the cash value of life insurance policies and annuities, which are protected against creditors and are excluded in the financial aid applications for college students.

Life insurance is also an effective way to create an instant legacy. By choosing beneficiaries selectively, a favorite charity may be supported, or a new charity even created. For example, after more than forty years of marriage, Preston and Nancy decided to review their philanthropic plans. Every year they supported various charities through donations, but as retirement neared, their focus shifted to future giving as opposed to current giving. With the projected reduction in their income during their retirement years, they didn't believe their cash flow would support continued contributions to various charitable organizations. So, instead, they looked at what they could do through their estate to help some charities with future gifts.

When examining their cash flow, Preston and Nancy identified a recurring expense going to premiums on a life insurance policy that had been purchased to replace income during their working years. With no dependents to support, they wondered if the premiums could be used in another manner. A couple of options surfaced for their consideration. The first option was to change the beneficiary on the policy to identify a specific charity. This option does not provide any income tax relief as a charitable donation, but it does allow for a future gift of the death benefit to the charity. Whether it is a church or university or other organization, naming that organization as the beneficiary would allow Preston and Nancy to fulfill a bequest with minimal involvement or paperwork.

Another option for them would be to approach a specific organization to seek cooperation in allowing the premium dollars currently being spent to instead be donated to the charity by naming the organization as the owner of the policy and as the beneficiary. If the organization agrees and establishes the proper framework as owner and beneficiary, the premiums paid to fund the policy become donations to the organization. Donations to a proper charity are tax deductible for

Preston and Nancy. Upon the insured's death, the organization receives the death benefit from the policy, and the couple has made both current and future donations to a charity.

Donations and gifts are important parts of estate plans. Whether you wish to leave something behind for relatives, make a donation to a favorite charity, or fund a foundation, doing so can be carefully outlined in your estate plan. Also important to consider is making financial gifts, particularly when such gifts will have a dramatic effect on your nest egg and your overall estate. We'll look at that next, in Chapter 24.

Lessons Learned

- Estate planning is not only for the wealthy. Anyone who wishes to preserve and protect assets for heirs and survivors should create an estate plan.
- Estate planning should incorporate such instruments as annuities, life insurance policies, and irrevocable trusts, all of which can help either defer or avoid taxes for the named beneficiaries.
- Life insurance can be used to create a legacy of charitable giving or even launch a new charity. Different options provide different avenues for ensuring that your favorite causes receive the benefits you would like them to have upon your death, without having to sacrifice the income you need during your retirement years.

CHAPTER 24

Budget Carefully for Financial Gifts

In previous chapters we've looked at how various couples and families crafted their estate plans so that they could leave financial gifts and make donations as they wished. Annuities, life insurance policies, and irrevocable trusts are among the financial tools that can help craft an estate plan that allows retirees both to live comfortably during their golden years and to leave something behind for the people and causes they care about.

Many of us want to make financial gifts to those we leave behind, although knowing when, how, and why to do so can be challenging. Such was the case for Adelaide.

Adelaide lost her loving husband more than fifteen years ago, after a he suffered a massive heart attack. He had been retired for only five years after having worked thirty-eight years at Widget Corporation as a plant supervisor. They only got a taste of what their dream retirement should have been.

Now 81 years old, Adelaide was recently uprooted from her lifelong family home and lives with her son and his family in Oregon. While she loves all of them, this is not how Adelaide envisioned her retirement. Let's just say that for six people ranging from ages 14 to 81 to live in tight quarters is not ideal.

Adelaide's unfortunate situation came about partly due to some circumstances that were out of her control and partly due to some poor decisions. It all started when Ben died unexpectedly. Although not wealthy, they had been enjoying a comfortable retirement. Between Social Security and the income provided by his lump-sum pension distribution, they had enough to live comfortably and still visit their three children, who are scattered around the country. After Ben died, Adelaide's income dropped slightly because of an adjustment to her Social Security income, but there seemed to be enough money each month to pay all her bills and still have some left over to spoil the grandchildren.

Adelaide's problem started with the beginning of the Great Recession in 2008. With the collapse of the stock market and plummeting interest rates, the monthly income from her investments dropped from $1,300 to barely more than $600. This left a sizable hole in her budget.

To make matters worse, Adelaide's son-in-law, Greg, lost his job and was on the verge of losing the house he shared with Adelaide's daughter and grandchildren because of the debts he and his family had accumulated. Seeing the desperate situation her daughter and two grandchildren were in, Adelaide couldn't just sit by and do nothing, so she loaned them $40,000 until they got back on their feet.

Unfortunately, it took Greg more than two years to find another job, so Adelaide loaned them an additional $30,000. These loans further reduced Adelaide's monthly income, so much so that she was having trouble paying her own monthly bills. Greg's new job didn't pay nearly as much as his previous one, so their repayments on the $70,000 in loans were few and far between.

The crippling blow came shortly thereafter when she learned that her son, Don, was also in financial dire straits. Don and his wife owned a small, specialty grinding company that provided parts to the automotive industry. Their business was cyclical: in good times, they made a lot of money, but in lean years, they barely broke even.

The 2008 recession was by far the worst of their lean years. They had to lay off more than half of their employees, and they had to borrow heavily just to pay the bills. By late 2009, the banks had called their loans, and with no new sources to borrow from, it looked like they would have to file for bankruptcy. What Don needed was a short-term loan to help him get through these tough times. If he could just pay off his largest loan, it would give him enough breathing room until things improved. Faced with losing everything they had worked for, Don approached Adelaide for a loan.

At first Adelaide hesitated, fearing that she wouldn't be able to pay her own bills if her income was reduced any further. Don assured her that he would pay monthly interest on the loan, and suggested that because he was willing to pay her 7 percent interest, her monthly income would actually go up. With his promise, and the potential to increase her income, she agreed to lend Don the $250,000 he needed. This left Adelaide with less than $50,000 in the bank.

At first things looked promising. Don was making the loan payments as promised, so Adelaide's monthly income did increase, giving her some day-to-day financial relief. What she didn't realize, though, was that Don's business was not improving. As a matter of fact, things were getting worse.

After another year of struggling, Don finally had to shutter the business. To add insult to injury, he had to get a job working for one of his competitors. One of the hardest conversations Don ever had was when he had to tell his mom that her money was gone. Between the tears, there was a lot of guilt and shame.

It was at this point that the family decided that the best option would be for Adelaide to sell her home in Cleveland and move in with Don and his family. Unfortunately, the recession had also ravaged the value of her home in the modest, middle-class neighborhood where she had spent the past fifty years. But, left with the proceeds of her home and the money she still had in the bank, she would have enough be able to contribute toward her son's household expenses and still have a few dollars left over at the end of the month.

While everyone in the family was pleasant toward her, she couldn't help but feel the occasional tension, and at times even some resentment that she was intruding on their lives. Unfortunately Adelaide really didn't have any other options. This was certainly not how she had envisioned her golden years.

Sometimes the heart is more generous than the wallet can afford. There are many Adelaides who have learned this bitter lesson.

Most people encounter some tough times in their lives, and somehow they get through them without having to ask for financial help. The trouble is, when we see someone struggling, especially if it involves our children or grandchildren, our instinct is to jump in and help them.

When faced with a situation in which you feel compelled to help someone financially, make sure you ask some critical questions:

- Is the person going through a tough situation or are they truly desperate? Simply going through a tough situation can build character and help cure bad financial habits.
- Have they done everything possible to reduce their spending, or are you just going to be supplementing their chosen lifestyle? Before you step in to help financially, consider suggesting that they trim their expenses.
- What exactly is the money going to be used for? This will give you a better idea if it's for a must-have or a nice-to-have.
- Can you afford to lose the amount you are lending? When lending money to relatives, it is best to consider it a gift since, more often than not, such loans are never repaid.
- What impact will lending money have on your own finances, including your monthly cash flow? Think twice before lending so much money that you sacrifice your own lifestyle.

If you do find yourself in a situation in which you decide to financially help one of your children, don't feel compelled to be "fair" to your other children. Giving an equal amount to your other children in the interest of fairness could only compound the problem. Giving money to someone when they don't need it might encourage them to spend it on something frivolous. Plus, if later on they do face financial difficulties, you've already given them money, which they've already spent. If being fair is an issue, instead of making equal gifts to your other children, consider addressing financial gifts in your will through an inheritance for your children or grandchildren. Always make sure your wallet can afford what your heart is telling you to do.

It can be challenging to plan for and budget for your retirement years. Many retirees face situations in which unexpected financial needs arise, whether crises that affect their children or themselves. Such crises can take a big bite out of retirement nest eggs. One of the biggest issues we face are health-related crises. We'll look at that next, in Chapter 25.

Lessons Learned

- When helping out family members financially, it's important to structure such help as a loan with interest. Know that there could be tax and legal implications on inter-family loans.
- When gifting or loaning money to family, make sure that you aren't depleting your own nest egg. Avoid giving away so much money that covering your own day-to-day living expenses becomes difficult.
- Be careful about being "fair" when loaning money to one family member and then gifting money to others so that no one feels either favored or cheated. Consider restricting financial gifts to inheritances outlined in your will and estate plan.

CHAPTER 25

Understand Your Government Benefits

When it comes to thinking about our golden years, many of us presume that we will be able to take advantage of Medicare and Social Security, two government programs that have long been part of the social fabric of America. Although most of us likely will rely on one or both of these programs, at least to some extent, during our retirement years, few of us truly understand all the rules and regulations that govern them.

Government programs are complex, and Medicare is a prime example of government complexity. Established in July of 1965, Medicare is a national insurance program administered by the U.S. government under Title XVIII of the Social Security Act to provide health insurance to people age 65 and older, regardless of income or medical history. During the past five decades, the provisions have been expanded to include benefits for speech, physical, and chiropractic therapy; payments to health maintenance organizations; payments for younger people with permanent disabilities who are receiving Social Security Disability Insurance payments; payments for those suffering from end-stage renal disease; almost all prescription drugs; hospice benefits; and treatment for amyotrophic lateral sclerosis (ALS, or Lou Gehrig disease).

The coverage is broad, so it can be difficult to understand all the rules and regulations. It's easy to get frustrated with Medicare and its copious rules and regulations, especially when we're affected personally, either in terms of the medical coverage it provides or the cost of the Medicare coverage itself.

A recent change in the cost of Medicare coverage, enacted by Congress in 2007, added means testing, or income-adjusted premiums, to how much seniors pay for Medicare Part B and Part D. According to a Kaiser Family Foundation report[15], 50.8 million seniors pay for Part B, the voluntary program that covers physician expenses. Of that group, 6 percent (2.9 million) pay higher, income-adjusted Part B premiums. The government enacted the same type of premium surcharges to Medicare Part D, the prescription drug plan offered by the government. According to the same study, fewer seniors participate in Part D, an estimated 42.4 million, and only 2.1 million of them (about 5 percent) pay the higher, income-adjusted Part D premiums. Here are a couple examples that illustrate how this new change can affect the unsuspecting.

Jack had been ill for many years, so the family was prepared for when the time finally came that he passed away. However, just before Jack died, he and his family had been surprised by a little-known fact about Medicare.

In 2006, before they officially retired, Jack and Katie purchased a retirement condominium, financing a portion of the purchase amount. Unfortunately, soon after retirement, Jack and Katie began to have financial issues. So, when interest rates dropped, they investigated refinancing the loan, hoping to reduce the monthly payment. However, because of the Great Recession in 2008–09, their retirement property values had dropped.

Jack and Katie soon learned that they no longer had equity in the property. They were prepared to ride it out and wait for the property value to recover, but they became very concerned about Jack's rising medical bills as his health began to deteriorate. They realized that they

---

15   Centers for Medicare & Medicaid Services, "Medicare Advantage 2015 Spotlight: Enrollment Market Update," June 30, 2015. Retrieved September 26, 2015, from http://kff.org/medicare/issue-brief/medicare-advantage-2015-spotlight-enrollment-market-update/

could no longer afford the condominium, so they concluded that they needed to try selling it for a price that would pay off the mortgage.

Unfortunately, with the economic recovery years away and no equity in the condominium, they soon learned that they were not going to be able to sell it for enough money to pay for the outstanding mortgage. So they consulted with the bank and decided to do a short sale. A short sale allows the owner of a property, to sell the property back to the bank and walk away from the debt. While they were disappointed to have to give up a portion of their retirement dream, getting rid of the mortgage provided instant financial relief to Jack and Katie, as Jack's deteriorating health resulted in even more medical bills. About six months after the short sale was completed, Jack passed away.

It was when Katie met with her tax preparer after Jack's death that she was caught off guard. She was still grieving from the loss of her husband when she learned that the difference between the appraised value of the condominium and the previous outstanding debt, which was forgiven by the bank, was defined as "imputed income" and was actually taxable income to her. Imputed income can also be incurred in a few other ways, among them by forgoing rental income on a property you own and live in.

As a result, Katie was going to have to pay taxes on money that she and Jack never even had. Furthermore, when this additional taxable "income" was added to Jack's pension income and her Social Security benefits, their adjusted gross income (AGI) now exceeded the threshold for the base Medicare Part B premiums. Consequently, instead of paying $104.90 per month, Katie had to pay $146.90. To make matters worse, since the government looks at IRS tax returns from two years ago, Katie was going to have to pay the increased premium for one year, meaning she would pay an additional $504 over that period. So, in addition to losing her husband, the condominium, and her Social Security benefits (she retained Jack's Social Security as his was the higher amount), she would have to pay taxes on income she never realized and she would have to pay more for Medicare for a full year—all because of a short sale that she really didn't want to do in the first place.

Medicare surprises like this are not as uncommon as one might think. Fred and Martha were both successful corporate managers. They loved their jobs and lived below their means, saving more than enough to support the retirement lifestyle they desired. Fred was three years older than Martha, and they planned to retire when Fred was 68 and Martha was 65, so they would both be covered by Medicare.

When Fred turned 65, he continued to work, and he signed up for Medicare Part A and B, like most senior citizens do. However, just as Fred turned 66 and Martha was 63, Martha's job was eliminated. Since she had worked for the company for more than fifteen years, she received a lump-sum severance package. The severance package pushed their combined AGI to more than $225,000 that year, causing each of their Medicare Part B premiums to rise from $104.90 to $209.80 per month, totaling an additional $2,517.60 over the next year.

Both Fred and Martha had pensions, so after they retired, between the pensions and other taxable income, their combined taxable income would exceed $170,000, resulting in each of them having to pay an additional $42 per month for Medicare coverage, theoretically for the rest of their lives (or at least until the next change in the Medicare laws).

Since changes in Medicare premiums often go unnoticed by most of us, many people learn about them only after a substantial income event has taken place. At that point, they typically don't have any chance of avoiding the increased premiums that result from certain financial windfalls. They simply have to live with it. Although income-adjusted premiums do not affect the majority of Americans, when it does, it catches them off guard, not unlike it did for Katie and for Fred and Martha.

If, like the folks in these examples, you are in a situation where you will be receiving a significant lump sum of money (such as a bonus, severance package, short sale, sale of investment property, or sale of a business), you may be able to restructure the transaction in order to minimize the impact on your taxable income, which can affect your Medicare premiums. For example, you might ask that a lump-sum payment or bonus be postponed until the following year or split over two years in order to potentially lower the impact on the current year. Although it might be difficult to completely avoid the additional charge, the impact could be reduced with some preparation.

Retirement planning should, of course, incorporate more than Medicare. Social Security also is an important to take into consideration. For many Americans, it is a primary source of retirement funds and has been for generations.

President Franklin D. Roosevelt signed the Social Security Act on August 14, 1935, and regular, ongoing, monthly benefits began to be paid to qualified workers in January of 1940. Since then, Social Security has been providing income benefits to individuals who have worked at least forty quarters (equivalent to ten years) and are at least 62 years old. In addition, there are benefits for survivors and disabled individuals under certain conditions, potentially prior to age 62.

Social Security benefits are based on an individual's lifetime earnings from the thirty-five years during which the individual earned the most. A formula is applied to arrive at the base benefit, or "primary insurance amount," which is what the individual will receive at "full retirement age," between ages 65 and 67, depending on the year of birth. Benefits can be accessed as early as age 62, though the government uses a formula to reduce benefits by approximately 6 percent per year when taken before full retirement age. Delaying the start of the benefit past full retirement age can increase the benefit by approximately 8 percent per year. It is best to contact your local Social Security Administration office to verify your exact benefits before you make the decision as to when to start collecting benefits.

For most Americans, Social Security is the main income source for retirement. Given the flexibility in the starting date of Social Security benefits as described above, the biggest issue for most individuals and couples as they approach retirement is when to start taking the benefits. And the best answer to that question is that it depends—on a lot of factors. For instance, starting to take Social Security at age 62, which is considered early retirement, can significantly reduce the monthly benefit. But in some cases, this might make a lot of sense. In other cases, it might be better to wait until age 70, which is the latest you can begin to take Social Security to maximize your benefits. Deciding when to begin drawing Social Security is not always as simple as it might seem.

Gary and Liz are retired. Gary loved his work and did not plan on retiring until age 70. He and Liz had worked with a financial planner, and Gary was aware that he could maximize his Social Security benefits if he did not start taking them until age 70. Delaying benefits also provided the couple with some income insurance in the event of a premature death of either one as the survivor would inherit the higher Social Security benefit for the rest of his or her life.

They were both healthy, didn't smoke, and expected to live a long time. Together, Gary and Liz had also done an excellent job of saving for retirement, ensuring that they had enough money to support the retirement lifestyle they wanted to lead. So, when Gary retired at 70, he started taking his Social Security payments immediately. Liz was at her full retirement age of 66, so she started her benefits at the same time. Everything was going as planned.

Unfortunately, at age 71, one year after starting his Social Security benefits, Gary discovered that he had pancreatic cancer. He died a year later. Liz, of course, was devastated emotionally, but she also became upset when she thought about how they had planned their long retirement, maximizing Gary's Social Security benefit to support that long-term plan.

Ironically, when Liz reviewed her financial situation, she realized that they had in fact done the right thing after all. Gary was the breadwinner, while Liz had taken an interruption in her career to raise four wonderful children before returning to work. Because of this job interruption, there was a significant disparity in their Social Security benefits. After Gary died, Liz remembered the plan, that she inherited his Social Security benefit, but lost hers, as Gary's was the greater of the two. And because Gary had worked until age 70, she was receiving the highest benefit possible. Even though it came at the loss of her husband, their financial plan had in fact protected her for the rest of her life.

The same cannot be said for Joe and Sally. Joe had a manufacturing job, and, when his company offered him an early retirement package, he took it. At age 61, he found himself at home with nothing to do. His wife was still working, they had family health insurance through her employer, and they had sufficient money coming in between her income and his pension, which had started immediately upon his early retirement.

A year later, Joe picked up some of his old hobbies, including golf and woodworking, so his expenses started to increase. When he turned 62, Joe felt it made sense to start his Social Security benefits to supplement his pension and Sally's income. Sally was the same age as Joe, and she planned to retire at age 65 when they both would be on Medicare.

The couple had two children, and Sally had significantly reduced her work hours while raising the children before returning to full-time work for the past ten years. As a result, her Social Security benefits were significantly lower than Joe's.

Three years later, Sally retired as planned and started her Social Security benefits at age 65. Life was good. They had Joe's Social Security, Joe's pension, and Sally's Social Security. Sally had not made nearly as much as Joe during her career, and she learned that she qualified for spousal benefits, which are typically 50 percent of the other spouse's income and are paid in addition to the other spouse's Social Security payments. The amount is adjusted by the age of the spouses when they start taking benefits (check with the Social Security Administration for specific details regarding the calculation of these benefits).

Here was the issue: Joe had longevity in his family. He was 61 when he retired, and both of his parents were still alive. He felt that he had a long time to live, so when it came time to select his pension, he chose the highest amount: single life. That meant that he would receive the highest amount as long as he was alive, but there was no provision for Sally after his death. Since he had taken the highest pension amount and he expected to live a long time, he felt that taking the lower Social Security benefit, starting at age 62, made sense. The extra money allowed Joe and Sally to live comfortably in retirement.

Unfortunately, Joe was playing golf one day and had a heart attack on the golf course. By the time they got him to the hospital, he had passed away. He was only 67. Obviously, Sally was distraught, but what added salt to the wound was when she found out that Joe's pension and her Social Security benefits stopped immediately upon his death, leaving her with only one income source, Joe's Social Security.

What neither Joe nor Sally had realized is that once a spouse dies, Social Security only continues to pay out one benefit, whichever is the higher of the two payments. Although Joe's benefit was the larger of the two, since he had started his Social Security benefit early at age 62, his benefit ended up being about 25 percent less than the amount that he would have received at his full retirement age of 66. That left Sally with only about 40 percent of the income that she and Joe had been living on before his untimely death.

Although many Americans depend solely on Social Security for their retirement lifestyle, Social Security alone isn't enough, just as Sally found out. In fact, according to *Your Social Security Statement*, prepared by the Social Security Administration:

> "Social Security is the largest source of income for most elderly Americans today, but Social Security was never intended to be your only source of income when you retire. You also will need other savings, investments, pensions or retirement accounts to make sure you have enough money to live comfortably when you retire."[16]

Knowing when to begin taking Social Security benefits is a tough decision. The beauty of life is that we never know what lies ahead of us. If we did, it would be all too predictable. However, not knowing what lies ahead makes planning for the future that much more difficult. As a result, deciding when it might be best to start Social Security benefits is not easy.

It's a good idea to plan for the worst case scenario and hope for the best. Good planning anticipates potential catastrophes and develops a strategy that can address them if they actually occur. Retirement can be a long-term proposition, though it can also be cut short. Since no one individual knows which it will be, it makes sense to anticipate both scenarios and balance them in order to provide and enjoyable retirement. We will discuss ways in which to plan for worst-case scenarios when it comes to long-term care issues, in Chapter 26.

---

[16]   Social Security Administration, "Your Social Security Statement," n.d. Retrieved on August 25, 2015, from http://www.ssa.gov/myaccount/materials/pdfs/SSA-7005-OL.pdf.

Lessons Learned

- Medicare and Social Security provide many Americans with helpful benefits that do much to supplement—if not wholly fund—their retirement income. But numerous rules and guidelines govern these programs, and so it is incumbent on everyone to understand how those rules will affect their retirement plans.

- Means testing, or income-adjusted premiums, affects how much seniors pay for Medicare Part B and Part D. As a result, it is important to calculate how pensions, Social Security benefits, and other income affect your adjusted gross income, which could mean a substantial difference in premiums.

- Knowing when to start taking Social Security benefits (and, if married, whose to take) can be challenging. It's important to factor in the differences in benefits when planning for retirement. Also important to consider is what will happen to benefits for the surviving spouse upon the death of the other.

CHAPTER 26

Play Defense During Retirement

Long-term care insurance should be on everyone's financial planning agenda. It's all too common for those who have eliminated debts, paid off the house, managed expenses, accumulated a comfortable nest egg, and planned carefully for retirement to still be sideswiped by unexpected healthcare expenses. Even those who are looking at a comfortable retirement with plenty of income to do whatever they want for what should be the rest of their lives can be clobbered by long-term care expenses, which can come raging in unexpectedly like a tornado, leaving finances in a wreck. Take for example what happened with Samuel and Sheila.

Samuel was one of the finest guys anyone could imagine: honest, caring, a genuinely good person. He had worked for the electric company his entire career as a repairman, retiring about eight years ago, at age 60, with a comfortable nest egg. Samuel was totally devoted to his wife Sheila, who loved children and worked part-time teaching at a Catholic school. They had been married more than forty years and were having a comfortable, relaxed retirement together, going on walks in their neighborhood, taking train trips around the country, and just generally enjoying each other's company.

The simple pleasures of life were the most important thing for Samuel, and he was careful not to spend too much from his savings so that it would last throughout their retirement years. Both he and Sheila had been frugal their entire lives; they had no debts, they were satisfied to go out just to inexpensive local eateries instead of fancy, pricey restaurants, and they opted to take driving trips to visit their children rather than elaborate vacations halfway around the world. At the rate they were going, Samuel and Sheila should have been comfortable for the rest of their lives. But an unfortunate turn of events rocked both of them to their core, changing their future forever.

Sheila had gone in for some back surgery several months earlier. It was supposed to be a simple, routine procedure. But several days later, something went wrong. Sheila started to feel paralysis creeping up her legs. She broke into a fever. She started feeling weak and had trouble breathing. She had to go back into the hospital, and then to a rehab facility, and then back into the hospital. Back and forth, in a vicious cycle. The doctors didn't know what the problem was. At one point, Sheila even slipped into a coma, and they didn't know if she'd ever come out of it. They were afraid there might be permanent brain damage. In another instance, doctors had to perform a tracheotomy. Shortly after that procedure, Sheila had severe trouble breathing.

It turned out that doctors had left stitches in her throat. In fact, it seemed like there had been a series of medical missteps. On several occasions, Sheila had come close to death. For months, she shuttled back and forth between hospitals and rehab facilities, coming home for only just a few days while all of this was happening.

Sheila finally managed to regain consciousness, and, luckily, there was no brain damage. But she remained bedridden, and there was serious doubt as to whether she could ever come home. It was far from clear whether she would ever be able to walk again. One way or another, Sheila was going to need extensive long-term care for the rest of her life. Seemingly overnight, both her life and Samuel's had been changed forever.

Not only was Samuel dealing with gut-wrenching grief over what was happening with his wife and all of her suffering—and how their entire future, the life they had planned together, was going to be entirely different from what they had hoped for and dreamed about—but there was something else. He had been figuring out how much Sheila's long-term care could cost them, and the yearly cost ran well into the six-figure range. It was frightening.

What Samuel began to recognize was the very real possibility that their financial nest egg could be severely depleted—or even completely wiped out—by the cost of Sheila's care. An entire lifetime's worth of accumulated assets could be vaporized in just a few years, which could ultimately leave both of them impoverished, with Samuel having nothing but his Social Security checks to live on.

Long-term care is something just about no one likes to think about. Most of us prefer to think about the sexy, exciting things surrounding financial and retirement planning like investing for long-term growth, building wealth, and watching a nest egg get bigger and bigger. It's much more pleasant to look at the balance sheet, chart its growth over the years, through market ups and downs, and feel a sense of accomplishment than it is to worry about what might happen if one or both spouses suffers a catastrophic health issue.

There's certainly a lot to be said for financial planning and weathering market ups and downs. That's what we call "playing offense" in the world of financial planning. But, similar to the world of sports, offense isn't all there is. There are two phases to the game: You've also got to play defense, and it's just as important as offense. That means that you've also got to think about the risks to your retirement security and take action to minimize and/or eliminate those risks if at all possible.

One of those risks is healthcare expenses. Most people are aware of this risk, and they take measures to have adequate health insurance in place to protect against these costs, which can be expensive, dangerous, and scary. Fortunately, once most people turn 65, they can count on Medicare to help with these costs. But what most people don't realize is that traditional health insurance covers only the costs incurred to treat conditions that are expected to improve in the future. In other words, it only covers things like surgeries and physical therapy treatments for illnesses that are expected to be temporary and that can and will get better with treatment.

But what about conditions that aren't expected to improve? What if someone needs help with things like eating, bathing, moving back and forth to the bathroom (known in the industry as "transference"), and other daily requirements? What if they need to be supervised because of a condition like Alzheimer dementia so they don't burn themselves on the stovetop, wander out into the street, or forget to take their medication?

In the financial planning and medical industries, these conditions are generally referred to as activities of daily living (ADLs). The basic six are eating, bathing, dressing, toileting, transferring, and continence. In many instances, these conditions are not expected to get any better. In other words, the patient's condition has stabilized or is slowly deteriorating, and he or she is going to need help with one or more ADLs for the rest of his or her life. In these situations, traditional health insurance will no longer cover these costs. If the doctor and/or other health professionals can't certify that the condition is expected to improve, traditional health insurance steps out of the picture. Most people are completely unaware of this, and they are shocked when they hear that their health insurance plan is going to stop covering these costs, which can be staggering.

Nursing home costs can easily run $80,000 per year or more. Those fees don't necessarily include the cost of doctors, nurses, or other trained personnel who might be required to provide care on an ongoing basis. In situations in which someone needs extensive around-the-clock care, the total yearly costs can easily run into the six-figure range.

No one likes the idea of going to a nursing home. But the concept of long-term care is actually much broader than that. If given a choice as to where to receive such care, most people would prefer to stay at home, in their natural and comfortable environment. Sometimes a spouse and/or adult children are available to help with care. But in today's mobile society, with children often scattered all around the country and families being smaller in the first place, relying on family to care for an ill and aged parent or sibling is often not an option.

For many people, the next best option is to hire people to come in and provide home healthcare if at all possible. In these cases, the healthcare providers charge on an hourly basis, and the total yearly cost can vary widely. If the patient needs help for only a few hours per week, the cost of home healthcare could be much less than care at a nursing home would be. But if the patient needs a lot of home care, especially from a licensed or registered nurse, the cost can actually be far higher, reaching more than double that of a nursing home, sometimes $150,000 a year or more.

Dorothy, for example, had been married for sixty-four years at the time of her husband's passing. She continued to live in the family house for another year after Sam died, but it became more and more difficult for her to remain in her home and keep it up all by herself. The family decided to move Dorothy into a nearby assisted living facility to provide for a better environment for her since she would have help with cleaning, laundry, and meals as well as around-the-clock medical assistance. Application was made to the facility, which included an evaluation by the facility's medical staff as well as Dorothy's primary care physician in order to determine the level of assistance needed. Dorothy was still capable of self-medicating, and, once in the new facility, her children assisted with the distribution of her medications by assembling her pill trays weekly and making sure her prescriptions were filled.

The family also tried to ease the transition by choosing familiar furniture that would accompany Dorothy to the facility. All she needed was her bedroom furniture, an easy chair, and a television. The more difficult task for the family was to get the house ready for sale and to dispose of the furniture, clothing, and kitchen, library, and garage items Dorothy no longer needed. It was difficult for Dorothy to come to terms with the disposition of the personal things she and her husband had accumulated over so many years of marriage together.

Nor was Dorothy's adjustment to living in the facility easy at first, as she continually asked when she could move back home. Despite the challenges with moving Dorothy, her children agreed that the assisted living facility was the appropriate place for their mother, and they wanted to be sure the transition was made carefully and lovingly.

Dorothy had enough retirement income to pay for most of the cost of the stay in assisted living, but she needed the money from the sale of the house to help. Dorothy's children discussed with her the need to sell the house, and she agreed it was the right thing to do—even though she didn't like the idea. It took almost a year for her house to sell. In the meantime, she used her savings to make up for the difference between her retirement income and her monthly rent.

The children had a financial durable power of attorney, a health care power of attorney, a living will, a do-not-resuscitate order, and a current will that had been drafted by an elder-care attorney shortly after Sam's death. The assisted living facility needed copies of all these documents for their files in order to be able to communicate effectively with the children.

Although it wasn't easy at first, right around one year into the transition, Dorothy was pleased with the facility, the meals, the staff, and her experience in general. Although the move had been made on relatively short notice, the family had for many years regularly discussed options for when a death or illness forced a decision to be made, which helped with Dorothy coming to terms with new living situation.

Statistics vary, but studies generally show that there is more than a 70 percent chance that of couples turning 65, at least one of them is going to need long-term care. So people who ignore this possibility risk exposing themselves to serious financial implications.

This means that even if you've spent years building up a nice portfolio in the hopes that it will provide enough income to fund a wonderful retirement lifestyle, the entire portfolio could be devastated by long-term care costs. All it takes is one spouse to be in need of long-term care over an extended period of time to deplete the entire nest egg, leaving both spouses impoverished.

Such is what happened to Ralph and Grace. Ralph was retired and had planned rather well for himself and his wife. They had their will, savings, investments, life insurance, and nursing home insurance all in place. Ralph's death preceded Grace's (as is often the case; husbands typically die before their wives). When Ralph died, it left Grace with all the decision-making tasks she had previously left up to him, including the financial decisions she hadn't been comfortable making. Grace was guided to an elder-care attorney to update all their financial documents, including her will, a revocable trust, a financial power of attorney, a health care power of attorney, and a living will. With her own retirement income, her survivor benefits from Ralph's pension, and her investment income, she seemed to be in a good place financially.

A few years after Ralph died, Grace began to experience some health-related issues. On a couple of occasions, she spent some time in a hospital, got rehabilitation therapy as a result of a couple of falls in her home, and also had to spend some time in a nursing home. Her nursing home insurance provided some help for the expenses incurred by Grace for her stays there, but she eventually exhausted the benefits provided by the insurance policy. When the nursing home insurance benefits ended, the cost of the nursing home became Grace's full responsibility. This meant that, since her retirement income alone would not cover the costs of her care, she would have to dip into savings and investments to pay the nursing facility so she could remain there and receive help.

Grace's recovery was slow, and her stay in the nursing facility extended from months to years. Her annual costs approached $90,000, and her savings began to drop due to the combination of withdrawals and low interest yields on her savings. In time her house was sold when it became clear that she wouldn't be leaving the nursing facility. Her savings continued to be drawn down to pay the costs of care. When she died, the assets she wished to bequeath to family and charity were minimal at best.

Grace's experience is not unusual. It appeared as if her finances were in order, and yet the family witnessed the gradual erosion of her estate due to the high costs of long-term care. What could have been done differently for Grace and her family in order to better protect her assets?

Grace had a nursing home policy, but because it was purchased in the 1980s, it was limited by the features available at the time the policy was issued, such as fewer months of coverage and lesser amounts of coverage in terms of dollars. In addition, Grace had some money in savings, but the low interest rates available in the past few years meant that the principal was spent more rapidly than interest was accruing as earnings couldn't keep up with rising costs of health care and rehabilitative care.

One of the things that most people commonly assume will help in this situation is Medicare, but unfortunately Medicare wasn't a reliable option for Grace, either. The fact is that Medicare is a form of traditional health insurance. Medicare generally does not cover long-term care costs. Once a situation gets to the point where a doctor can no longer certify, in writing, that the patient's condition is improving, Medicare steps out of the picture.

Medicaid is designed to step in and help in this situation, but because it is a means-based program. Means-based testing determines whether someone is entitled to financial-assistance so recipients have to meet strict eligibility requirements in order to qualify. In other words, you generally have to burn through your own assets first before Medicaid will provide support.

People are often surprised, and even upset, when they find out about this. They hear that they have to be broke to qualify for Medicaid, and they get angry. They think it's unfair. They think they're being penalized for being smart their entire lives, saving carefully, and putting together a nest egg. After all, they didn't have to do that; they could have been frivolous, neglected to save money, and spent everything they had on living a more extravagant lifestyle year after year, and then they wouldn't have the nest egg in the first place and so they would qualify sooner for Medicaid.

But that's just how it is. As it is, Medicaid costs are going through the roof. It's putting a huge strain on state budgets throughout the country. Resources are stretched to the limit, and no one seems amenable to raising taxes so that that funding is available to pay for long-term care for people who already have their own money. The public just doesn't want to do it. So until and unless the public has some sort of revolutionary change in attitude, it's not wise to expect this situation to change any time soon. Until then, Medicaid will remain primarily a welfare program for the poor.

In order to qualify for Medicaid, some couples consider transferring their assets to their children, a tactic referred to as "Medicaid planning." There are severe limitations to this, however. First, there's a five-year look-back period, meaning that assets given away during that period disqualify individuals for Medicaid for a certain time, depending on how much was given away. Second, certain assets are difficult and/or expensive to give away, such as IRAs and Roth IRAs. Transferring title to such assets cannot be done without paying immediate income tax on the entire balance, which is cost prohibitive in most cases. Finally, giving away assets also means relinquishing total control over them forever. This is an extremely unpalatable option for most people, who just can't bring themselves to pull the trigger when it comes time to do this.

With Medicare, the patient pays $0 for days 1–20, $157.50 per day for days 21–100, and 100 percent thereafter for hospitalization. Medicare does not pay for long-term care like Grace faced, because her stay went beyond 100 days. Medicare Part A (Hospital Insurance) might cover care given in a certified skilled nursing facility if it's medically necessary to have skilled nursing care (such as changing sterile dressings). However, most nursing home care is custodial care, including help with bathing or dressing. Medicare doesn't cover custodial care if that's the only care needed by the patient.

Furthermore, Grace would not have been eligible for Medicaid, the healthcare program for impoverished and low-income families and individuals, even as she continued to spend her savings, primarily because her retirement income exceeded the threshold for Medicaid eligibility, which requires income at or below the poverty level and assets of less than $1,500.

Fortunately, Grace and her family had done their homework in terms of having the typical legal documents in place and up to date, well in advance of Grace's illness. As Grace went through her decline in health, the financial power of attorney given to her son allowed the bills to be paid. The healthcare power of attorney allowed her daughter to communicate with the nursing facility in order to keep current with Grace's needs. The revocable trust that held Grace's non-IRA assets, created to avoid delays in distribution that could sometimes be caused by the process of clearing probate, was available to be used to pay for Grace's expenses. In other words, as much as could be done in advance was done to help Grace. The involvement of the family was critical in this situation to allow things to go as smoothly as possible.

For those who don't want to pay for long-term care insurance, there are other options, however, including to self-insure. This requires individuals to pay any healthcare costs out of pocket. Of course, it takes a rather large reserve to generate enough income to pay long-term care costs for an extended period, even just for one spouse, while at the same time generating enough income to afford the healthy spouse a decent retirement. For the vast majority of families, self-insuring is just not a viable option.

Even more extreme, some couples resort to divorce so that the healthy spouse's assets might no longer be subject to the long-term care costs of the ill spouse and a government program like Medicaid might take over. For most longtime married couples, this is an extremely unpalatable, if not inconceivable, course of action to take.

A more realistic option is to purchase long-term care insurance. Long-term care insurance limits the risk of debilitating healthcare costs to the cost of the premium and any deductibles. Any risk beyond that is borne by the insurance company. This can be a wise idea in many cases, because the yearly insurance premium likely won't change your retirement lifestyle or threaten your nest egg.

With long-term care insurance coverage, benefits are generally triggered whenever your doctor can certify that you need help with at least two ADLs. Once the benefits are triggered, a good policy typically will pay not just for a nursing home, but also for assisted living and even home healthcare. Long-term care insurance is often referred to as "antinursing-home insurance" because it can actually help you stay in your own home.

The level of benefits of long-term care insurance depends on the policy. Think of the benefit level as a shield: If you incur certain expenses, the shield will be there to absorb the blow, thereby protecting your other assets. How big the shield is depends on the scope of the policy. Of course, the bigger shield you choose, the more expensive the premium. A typical benefit level might be, say, $90,000 per year, for a total of three years, or a total shield of $270,000, providing a pool of money available to cover healthcare costs.

Determining how big a shield (that is, what kind of insurance policy) to pay for can be difficult. One rule of thumb is to remember that it's not necessary to buy a policy that covers the absolute worst possible case, such as an extended multiyear need for long-term care, but rather to get a reasonable amount of insurance that will at least give you some breathing room and has a decent likelihood of providing enough coverage in most cases.

Deciding on the size of a long-term care insurance policy is crucial, as is timing: You've got to get it when you still qualify for coverage. In other words, you have to make a conscious decision to get this insurance while you're still healthy enough to convince an insurance company to cover you. When applying for coverage, the insurance company is going to carefully examine your medical records, including a detailed medical questionnaire that assesses your health status, before deciding whether to offer coverage. Individuals who wait to apply for long-term coverage until it's actually needed find that this option is no longer on the table.

Many people don't realize this. Everyone seems to intuitively understand that you can't wait until you have a terminal cancer diagnosis and then apply for a huge life insurance policy or wait until you smell smoke in your house before you apply for homeowners insurance. But for some reason, a lot of people assume they can wait until they need a walker, or get macular degeneration, or start to forget who their children are before they need to consider getting long-term care insurance.

Unfortunately, it just doesn't work that way. In the case of long-term care costs, you've got to play defense by applying for the insurance while you're still healthy enough to get it. It might not be the most appealing thought in the world, it might not be as exciting as playing offense the way you did all your working life by spending a lot of mental and emotional energy on growing your nest egg in the first place, but it's essential to play defense. You've got to play both sides of the game in order to be successful.

Samuel had always shrugged off the idea of long-term planning insurance and decided not to do anything about it, mainly because he didn't like the idea of paying the premium. He had opted for a slightly higher retirement income every year, but in doing so left himself (and Sheila) totally exposed to the risk of long-term care expenses.

This required Samuel to restructure his assets and take other drastic measures such as using his investments and IRA assets to purchase income annuities in order to try to minimize the impact of the impending long-term care expenses. These measures were permanent and irreversible and could no longer be considered "countable resources," and thus were no longer subject to Sheila's long-term care expenses. Medicaid generally frowns on these types of techniques and has tried to challenge them, but taxpayers generally have prevailed in court decisions when using these tactics. Still, these are not moves that would be made in less extreme circumstances.

No one wants to face extreme circumstances during their retirement years. Even if it appears that you have a sound retirement plan in terms of having a good income stream for the rest of your life, and you're safely under the Medicare umbrella or have other health insurance for the cost of doctors, hospitals, and medications, the risk of long-term care expenses can still threaten your financial future. It's important for everyone to consider their options for how to mitigate this risk, including whether to get long-term care insurance.

Managing risk is a concern for almost everyone as they live out their retirement years. Trusts, life insurance, long-term care insurance, and other investment vehicles can help you preserve your assets and provide for survivors. In fact, preserving your assets, covering your end-of-life expenses, and planning your legacy are important aspects of retirement planning. We'll look at those next, in Chapter 27.

Lessons Learned

- Healthcare expenses can obliterate retirement nest eggs in just a few short years. Retirement planning should include long-term care planning for costs associated with healthcare issues such as surgery, physical therapy, nursing home care, and assisted living.
- Medicare and Medicaid can assist with healthcare expenses only up to a point. Medicare, for instance, does not cover long-term, life-threatening illnesses. In addition, Medicaid is a means-based program, and so often is of no or little help for retirees with sizable nest eggs.
- Long-term care insurance is a viable option to guard against healthcare expenses incurred during retirement—but it must be purchased before illness strikes. Those who wait until long-term care is needed will find it unlikely that they can purchase affordable long-term care insurance.

CHAPTER 27

Leaving a Legacy

The population of those older than 80 years of age is growing faster than any other segment, according to a 2015 United Nations report, and is a big part of the surge of Baby Boomers into what is sometimes called the "Silver Tsunami." As these individuals continue to grow older and enter their twilight years, it becomes even more relevant to address all the related issues of aging. Preparing a family to acknowledge and face elder-care decisions takes a commitment to communication. The decline of the mental or physical capabilities of an older loved one may take a long time to manifest itself. Once a pattern of behavioral or mental changes becomes clear, the family needs to get involved if it hasn't been already. Discussing the roles each family member will take is important. Identifying a plan of action should make it easier to deal with the changes. Being in communication with the family doctor, the family clergy, and anyone else with whom your elders have contact most likely will make the dilemma more manageable for all.

Unfortunately long-term care planning, discussed in the previous chapter, which should begin when people are in their fifties, is usually being addressed once they're in their seventies or later, after college educations are paid for and other retirement planning has taken place. Among the issues to consider are the expenses associated with nursing home and other long-term care. People want to know what can be done to try to reduce the potential exposure to out-of-pocket costs as applied to assisted living, nursing home, and at-home care expenses. Many times the trigger to initiating long-term care planning for the elderly is often onset of illness or the death of a spouse, which forces the surviving spouse and/or the family to make immediate decisions.

Buying long-term care and nursing home insurance as a way to try to protect against these risks became popular in the early 1970s. A lot has changed in the form of options, terms of coverage, and prices since the idea of insuring against nursing home expenses become available as a private pay policy as opposed to relying on government-sponsored insurance such as Medicaid. One thing that has remained an item of concern is the underwriting or qualifying for long-term care insurance, which comes in two forms: a health underwriting and a financial underwriting. Those may seem like obvious items, but understanding the difference is important.

Traditional long-term care and nursing home care requires an application for a policy with a premium that has to be paid monthly or annually. The premium will be based on how soon the benefit will commence (known as the elimination period), the length of the benefit period (two years, three years, five years, or lifetime), and the daily amount of coverage ($100, $150, $200, etc.), and whether it is an indemnity or reimbursement policy. An indemnity policy pays the daily amount regardless of expense, while a reimbursement policy pays the amount of the daily cost up to the limits of the policy. These types of policies favor younger, healthier applicants with incomes to support the premium payments.

One of the drawbacks of the traditional long-term care policy is the simple fact that if the policy is not used, the premiums are not recoverable unless the applicant is willing to pay what amounts to about a 50 percent increase to buy what's called the return-of-premium option. The return-of-premium option provides that if the policy is not used and claims are not made, the policy may be surrendered and premiums paid will be returned to the policy owner.

A more contemporary way to obtain long-term care insurance is with single premium purchases. This approach is more suitable for those with sufficient savings to be able redirect surplus dollars to an insurance company in order to obtain coverage in excess of what savings alone might provide. In these instances, is not unusual for the underwriting to be more favorable, in the simple form of four or five questions requiring a yes or no answer and a telephone interview with an underwriter to assess the applicant. This process, compared to the underwriting on life insurance, is often done in a shorter time frame. What could otherwise take months might be done in just a few weeks. An additional benefit of this approach is the control maintained over the money. If the need for a nursing issue doesn't arise, the money put into the premium remains available to use for other purposes, just as with any savings account, and it may pass to a beneficiary income tax–free as a life insurance settlement.

In addition to single-premium purchases, annuities can serve as another useful tool for covering long-term care expenses. Jim and Stella were both age 75 and had been married for more than fifty years. Both of them owned an annuity, which had been purchased with existing savings. Such savings are known as nonqualified dollars because no tax deduction is associated with the principal used to purchase the annuities. The annuities are tax-deferred instruments; the interest is taxed only when it is withdrawn from the annuity, and the principal is not taxed at withdrawal.

The annuities owned by each of them matured after the five-year term of the contract. Much like certificates of deposit available through a bank or credit union, an annuity has a specified term of deposit. At maturity, if Jim and Stella surrendered or cashed in the annuities, the interest earned from time of deposit, which had up to this point grown tax-deferred, would be fully reportable (on Form 1099) and taxable. Jim and Stella learned that annuities issued after 2010 that met certain standards would continue to grow tax-deferred earnings, but if the earnings were withdrawn to pay long-term care expenses, the withdrawal would be deemed income tax–free.

Jim and Stella, not wanting to pay taxes if it wasn't necessary, exchanged their old annuities under IRS Code Section 1035 and created new annuities on which, if used for long-term care, the earnings withdrawn would not be subject to income taxes. The principal in this instance was already nonqualified in the original purchase so there would be no taxable event for Jim and Stella as long as the annuities were used for long-term care expenses.

This solution was a relatively simple one for Jim and Stella, as it was for Betty, who became a widow at a relatively young age and had a number of financial concerns she wanted to address. Widowed and still single, she was financially comfortable with savings, investments, and survivor benefits from her husband's employer. She had a significant amount of savings but was still concerned about nursing home expenses. She also wanted to be able to leave money for her adult children after she died.

Betty applied for a single premium life insurance policy to try to accomplish three things: 1) to defer taxes on interest earned on the deposit; 2) to leverage the amount available for long-term care and, in effect, double the deposit; and 3), to preserve the deposit in the event she never used the money for long-term care (it then could be used for any reason, or it could pass to her beneficiaries on a tax-free basis). Betty used what was otherwise idle savings to boost her coverage for long-term care and obtain income tax relief without losing control of her money.

Due to changes in the laws regarding annuities and health care, there are more reasons today than ever before to investigate the various ways to use insurance, company-provided annuities, and life insurance to solve multiple needs. Reggie and Veronica, for example, wanted to address several issues. Both were in their early sixties, and they had been married for more than thirty-five years. They were interested in obtaining some insurance protection against the exposure to long-term related expenses, but they did not want to have an annual premium expense added to their budget. During the course of their investigation, they found that they could use an existing IRA to fund insurance against long-term care issues. Because of a job change years ago, Reggie had an idle IRA to which no additions were being made. They found that an IRA in Reggie's name could be split and redirected to a new IRA to try to get this coverage put in place. They decided to apply for this coverage, and so a life insurance application was completed for the purpose of determining if, as a couple, they were healthy enough to get the insurance issued.

They were approved. The next step was to request a trustee-to-trustee transfer of the existing IRA to the new IRA to be deposited into an annuity with the same insurance company that approved the life insurance application. With everything in place, the annuity in the IRA will make annual distributions that will be used to pay the premiums. Since the distributions will come from an IRA, taxes will be withheld and the after-tax payment will be made to the life insurance policy to make the premium payments necessary to keep the policy in force.

This process essentially transfers money from the IRA over several years, and what's left is a fully funded whole life insurance policy. The policy is the base for long-term care benefits, which will not be taxed when received if used for healthcare expenses.

Knowing that, Reggie moved $150,000 from his IRA at age 70 to provide fifty months of coverage in the amount of $4,226 per month for either himself or Veronica. Over a twenty-year period, $9,789 annually was sent from the IRA to the life insurance policy.

IRA accounts must begin distributing a minimum amount of income each year starting after the IRA owner reaches age 70½. The calculation needs to be done annually and is based on the value of the IRA and the age of the IRA owner. Reggie's situation more than fulfills the minimum distribution requirements and keeps the policy in force. Long-term care benefits are based on the face value (i.e., death benefit) of the policy and are received income tax-free. Because Reggie and Veronica were healthy enough for approval (meaning their height and weight were within limits set by underwriting), and because their medical history met the standards set by the insurance company underwriting, this process worked well for them. In other words, their use of tobacco and prescription drugs to control things like hypertension, cholesterol, diabetes, and the like were acceptable to the underwriter to allow for the issuance of the coverage.

Life insurance may be used in another matter that doesn't relate to long-term care but does help provide for the creation of an instant estate or to provide a legacy in the form of a trust or gift to a charitable organization. Dave and Jackie are in their mid-eighties and have been retired for more than twenty years. They have no concerns as it relates to their own income needs. There are no children or grandchildren in need of support, although they have donated to a favorite charity over the years with intermittent contributions. They would like to do something more significant now that their children have grown and have families of their own. So, Dave and Jackie would like to redirect some of the life insurance they've owned for years to their favorite charity. By merely changing the beneficiary on a policy, they can make a future gift to the charity. The gift could go to the charity's general fund, or it could be specified for a particular use or program. Without adding to their budget, Dave and Jackie have created an opportunity to leave a final and significant contribution to a charity that they hold dear.

In another instance, Rick and Catherine, both of whom are in their fifties and have been married for twenty years, are both still working. They wish to provide current and future financial support for a group for which they have long had a tremendous amount of respect. The couple applied for a joint life policy in the form of survivorship. As described in Chapter 23, the policy only pays out upon the second death. This makes sense for them because the underwriting is more likely to be approved even if one has a health issue which might change the underwriting for a traditional life insurance policy, since the policy pays at the second death, not the first, hence the name "last to die."

Once they are approved, their next step is to have the owner of the policy become the charity. At original application, ownership would have been in Rick's and Catherine's names as Health Insurance Portability and Accountability Act (HIPAA) rules stipulate that only they can answer health questions, which an entity couldn't do. Once approved and no further underwriting is needed, then an entity can be made the owner.

Rick and Catherine remain the insured and will make the premium payments. The premiums, made payable to the charity, become tax deductible to Rick and Catherine. The beneficiary is the charity, so Rick and Catherine can make a current contribution of support in the form of the premiums paid on the policy. In addition, upon the second death, a future gift will be received by the charity as the beneficiary.

Bequests to charity historically have been made through a will or similar device by a decedent, but for those without fortunes to disburse at death, a life insurance policy can have the same effect and allow for a lasting memory or an endowment.

In a similar role with respect to charitable giving, an individual has the option to designate money in an IRA to be used for charitable purposes. The Internal Revenue Service has held the position that an IRA is a retirement vehicle and not an estate-transfer device. That is why the IRA owner has to be sure to follow very specific guidelines about taking distributions from an IRA account at the specified times. There is a life expectancy table indicating how long you are expected to live once you reach a certain age. For example, let's say that at age 70 you are expected to live for another seventeen years; if you are calculating a joint life expectancy, then one of you will live for another twenty-seven years. It is the joint or uniform life expectancy that determines the required minimum distribution for IRA accounts. As such, an IRA owner must take 3.65 percent of the IRA for the initial required minimum distribution (RMD).

IRAs allow for the creation of savings and for the deferral of income taxes while the account accumulates earnings. At age 70½, the IRA owner must begin taking withdrawals, or RMDs, as previously mentioned. Failure to take the distributions is subject to an excise tax of 50 percent of what the distribution should have been. Every year, the custodian of the IRA account sends out Form 5498, which notifies the IRS of the December 31 value of the previous calendar year. This is important because the RMD is based on the December 31 value of your IRAs. Since technically the RMD doesn't need to begin until April 1 of the year after reaching age 70½, there is time to initiate the RMD. Generally, it is best to take the first distribution requirement by December 31 because if the distribution is held until April 1, it counts against the previous year and another distribution must be completed by December 31 to avoid the excess tax penalty of 50 percent.

Some find that taking the RMD is not ideal. If the income is not needed, why take the money, pay the taxes—and then do what with the proceeds? Reinvestment is a possibility, as is making contributions to charity. Gifts to grandchildren into a College Savings 529 plan might be another good alternative. If you wish to take the distribution and not pay taxes, consider making a gift directly to a charity of up to $100,000 from the IRA to meet the RMD. This is not recorded as a charitable deduction because it goes directly to the charity and is therefore not included in the gross income for the taxpayer.

There are many interesting and diverse ways in which people can leave a lasting legacy, not just for your family, but also organizations and charities that you are passionate about. Don't overlook some of the various ways that can allow you to fulfill your long-term financial goals.

Lessons Learned

- Long-term care planning should take place when you're in your fifties, ideally alongside retirement planning, rather than in your seventies or eighties, when health-related issues might force healthcare costs to increase.

- In addition to considering the financial implications of long-term care, elders and their families also should put in place a financial durable power of attorney, a health care power of attorney, a living will, a do-not-resuscitate order, and a current will.

- Life insurance and IRAs are among the financial instruments that can be used to fund long-term care expenses, charitable giving, college savings plans, and financial legacies, and they should be considered part and parcel of elder-care planning.

Conclusion

We hope that reading this book has inspired and motivated you to get your own financial house in order, regardless of its current condition. Some will walk away feeling pretty good about their situation and have the confidence that their financial plan needs only minor adjustments. Others may look at their situation and have no idea of where to even begin. For the latter, I'll share with you a quote I heard years ago: "How do you eat an elephant? One bite at time!"

In the book we covered the gamut of financial issues that many people face at different stages of their lives. We discussed the value of budgeting and saving, prudently managing debt and student loans, saving for specific goals such as college and retirement, investing wisely in an irrational world, knowing how much you can afford to spend in retirement, and using insurance to better manage the many risks that life throws at us.

In addition we covered several special situations such as dealing with a divorce, losing a loved one, avoiding financial scams, and assisting someone with a financial need.

We explored the importance of having all your estate planning documents in order, while you are living and also when you are gone. It is critical for loved ones to know what your specific wishes are in the event you are incapacitated or pass away.

Proper financial planning is truly a cradle-to-grave enterprise that needs to be carefully coordinated and implemented. The whole process covers a number of different disciplines and may involve several different professionals including attorneys, accountants, investment advisors, and insurance agents. For many people this is where the wheels fall off. The prospect of dealing with so many issues and people, and trying to coordinate all of their recommendations, may be enough to freeze someone into paralysis. People who never meet their financial goals don't plan to fail, they simply fail to plan.

Creating the financial legacy you envision results from successful planning, which is a four-step process:

1. Set realistic goals.
2. Develop a detailed plan to meet those goals.
3. Implement the plan.
4. Periodically make adjustments.

First you need to make sure your goals are realistic and attainable. This is where financial advising can be invaluable. A trustworthy financial advisor will initially review your situation from a wide perspective. The only way to accurately assess the situation is by "running the numbers." The calculations need to be not only accurate, but also realistic. Many people feel they are falling short of their goals because their assumptions were too aggressive or optimistic, setting them up for disappointment. Typically you and the advisor will want to run several different scenarios to see what the range of possible outcomes may be. The exercise will give you an idea of how vulnerable your desired outcomes may be to certain variables such as overestimating your assumed rate of return on your investments or underestimating the impact inflation may have on your future purchasing power.

After you have determined that your goals are realistic, you then need to develop your specific list of tasks that need to be done. Setting up a priority list can help reduce the anxiety of trying to do it all at one time. Like we said earlier—one bite at a time. From there, you can focus on the action items that need immediate attention, and create a plan for addressing the ones that can wait.

After the priority list is established, the next step is to determine what needs to be done to meet your goals. This is where prioritizing can be beneficial. Going through your list, some of the tasks can be straightforward, such as increasing your 401(k) contributions, paying

MONEY TALKS: *Life Lessons to Help You Plan Now, Save Wisely, and Retire Well*

down your credit card debts more aggressively, or using a health savings account at work. Others may require more thought or additional effort, and possibly the involvement of additional professionals, such having a will or trust drafted.

The next step in the financial planning process is a critical one—you actually have to implement it! While the importance of implementing your plan sounds obvious, many people drop the ball at this point. With all of our collective years of experience, we have run across scores of people who have gone through the exercise (and cost!) of having a detailed professional financial plan developed for them, only to have it sitting in a binder years later covered in dust. The final goal is not to have a great plan drawn up, but rather to enjoy its results. As many of us have heard growing up, "The road to hell is paved with good intentions."

Implementing a financial plan can be complex at times, especially when some of the recommendations may appear to be contradictory. Again, this is where the role of a trusted financial advisor may be critical in establishing the priorities for implementation and sorting out any inconsistencies. An effective financial plan has to be executed accurately and on a timely basis.

The difference between a goal and a dream is the amount of effort put behind it, and the time you take to review your progress periodically. The final step in the financial planning process is to periodically revisit the plan and make any required adjustments. While we may not like it at times, change is inevitable. Markets will go up and down, and your job or personal situation may change. Keeping up with these changes and making adjustments will go a long way in making sure you are still on track to success. Many times we have seen people get into financial difficulties because they failed to make the necessary adjustments to an event that life threw at them. The key to financial success is to learn to adapt to change.

The four-step financial planning process is a proven formula, which will help ensure you achieve your financial goals. The key is following the process. Although it is simple, it is not necessarily easy. If it was, everyone would be successful. It takes hard work, time, and discipline, but the rewards more than make up for the sacrifices. And for those who don't feel comfortable or up to the challenge, seek out your own trusted financial advisor who can help you develop, implement, and adjust your own successful plan.

Having taken the time to read this book, will you simply put it on a shelf and forget about it? Or will you begin the process with some proactive steps today that will help assure that you meet your own financial goals? Numerous studies have shown that when people decide to make a change in their lives, if they immediately take even a few small steps they dramatically increase their chances of meeting their goals. Our hope is you have taken this as your own personal wake up call to get your financial house in order!

So, what will you do now?

Contributors

Chuck Conrad

 Chuck is a Senior Financial Planner at Szarka Financial, holds a juris doctor degree, and specializes in transition planning, whether it results from the loss of a job, a loved one, or a relationship. Chuck routinely advises entrepreneurs who are purchasing franchises or starting their own consulting business. He currently appears on WJW Fox8 as a financial expert.

Prior to joining Szarka Financial, Chuck was a Financial Advisor at both Smith Barney and Merrill Lynch. Chuck also spent several years in the private practice of law with the estate planning and tax group of Chattman, Gaines & Stern in Cleveland, Ohio, and was a judicial extern for the Honorable Judge John Donnelly of the Cuyahoga County Probate Court.

His background also includes several years of active military duty, serving in the Army's 82nd Airborne Division during the first Gulf War.

Chuck has four daughters and resides in Lakewood, Ohio.

Rick Martin

Rick is a Certified Financial Planner™ at Szarka Financial, and since 2000 has focused on assisting people to identify their long-term financial goals and to develop a plan to balance those goals with the investment risk they may need to take. He currently appears on WJW Fox8 as a financial expert.

Rick spent more than 25 years with National City Bank, Progressive Corporation, and Cole National Corporation. A cancer survivor, Rick knows how important it is to develop contingency plans for unanticipated emergencies such as the loss of a job, major health issues, long-term disability, or premature death. His experience surviving cancer, being in business, using the services of a major brokerage firm, and now financial planning gives Rick a unique perspective into the issues that face his clients.

Rick and his wife Emily have four children, and live in Orange Village, Ohio.

Alex Menassa

Alex is a Senior Financial Planner at Szarka Financial, a CPA, and holds a juris doctor degree, along with a master's degree in business administration with a focus in taxation. Specializing in tax and estate planning issues related to IRAs, since 1999 he has put together financial plans for families that integrate investment, tax, estate-planning, and asset-preservation strategies into coherent, effective programs to achieve their objectives. Alex is known for his ability to convey complex ideas in a remarkably clear, simple, and understandable fashion that people can easily relate to their own lives. He currently appears on WJW Fox8 as a financial expert.

Prior to joining Szarka Financial, Alex worked with the Private Banking group at KeyBank, which specialized in planning for high-net-worth clients. As a CPA, he focused his time on research projects related to tax planning, estates, trusts, and corporations.

Alex has two children and resides in Wadsworth, Ohio.

Mark Stratis

Mark is a Certified Financial Planner™ at Szarka Financial, providing guidance and consultation in the areas of insurance, holistic financial planning, and tax-efficient investment management, and has been working with individuals and small business owners since 1979. He currently appears on WJW Fox8 as a financial expert.

His passion is to help people focus on accumulating money, saving on taxes, and generating better returns on existing dollars, by providing common-sense solutions to everyday financial situations.

Mark has been a district manager at IDS/American Express where he trained advisors. He managed a branch office for a regional brokerage firm, and a district for a national life and health insurance company. He conducted various tax planning and management courses for CFP® candidates across the country until 1990, when Mark founded Stratis Asset Management. He joined Szarka Financial in 2010.

Mark has a son, and lives with his wife Debbie in Hudson, Ohio.

Les Szarka

Les is the author of *Money Brain: How Your Subconscious Mind Can Hijack Your Investment Decisions* and Chief Executive Officer, founder, and co-owner of Szarka Financial. He has been a financial advisor and retirement planning specialist for over 30 years.

Les currently appears on WJW Fox8 as a financial expert. He also appeared for several years as a financial correspondent on the television show *Golden Opportunities* on NBC Channel 3 WKYC. Les has appeared in *The Wall Street Journal*, Fox Business, *Crain's Cleveland Business*, *The Cleveland Plain Dealer*, and *Inside Business*.

Les is a Certified Financial Planner™, a Chartered Financial Consultant, and a Registered Securities Principal through FSC Securities Corporation. He is also a member of the Financial Planners Association (FPA).

Les and his wife Debbie reside in Westlake, Ohio.

89482594R00116

Made in the USA
Lexington, KY
29 May 2018